Two Years

Quest for Money, Purpose, and Love

Max Tower

Max Tower is the pen name for his eye-opening travel memoir Two Years. In the past, Max worked in investment banking across Frankfurt, London, and New York until he reached the point where he was longing for something more meaningful. He quit his job and ego-identity to embark on a two-year journey around the world, during which he learned to approach life from an entirely new perspective. For that, Max switched from rationality, logic, and numbers to feeling, trust, and intuition. A 180-degree change to life.

Tag along on his adventures at *www.two-years.com.*

Copyright © 2023 Max Tower. All rights reserved.

The content within this book may not be reproduced, duplicated, or transmitted without direct written permission from the author or the publisher.

Under no circumstances will any blame or legal responsibility be held against the publisher, or author, for any damages, reparation, or monetary loss due to the information contained within this book, either directly or indirectly.

Published by Mindstir Media, LLC
45 Lafayette Rd | Suite 181 | North Hampton, NH 03862 | USA
www.mindstirmedia.com

Printed in the United States of America
ISBN: 978-1-961532-65-6

Let go.

Trust.

Receive.

Contents

Introduction	7
Life in Society	13
Breaking Out	25
Quest for Money	35
Quest for Purpose	55
Quest for Love	123
The Grand Finale	175
Closing Remarks	211
References	217

Introduction

Do you know the feeling of being stuck in your life? That you have achieved everything the external or material world has to offer? And that you are seeking something more meaningful? Each one of us will have to face that exact feeling at some point in our lifetime. We have lived our lives in conformity with society's standards and should theoretically be satisfied with what we have or have achieved: Good degrees, a more or less satisfying job, house and car, close circle of friends, and maybe our own family. Yet we feel that something is missing. That we are not whole. We might be able to suppress those feelings and emotions for a while with even more external distractions, but we will ultimately come back to where we started. We realize that a life from the ego-perspective is no longer sufficient; therefore, we need to look for answers elsewhere. The journey inward commences.

We want to understand what life is about. Why we are here on this planet. What our purpose is. What unites us all. However,

Introduction

nobody taught us in school, at work, or in sports clubs how we should approach this phase of our life. What we are "trained" for is to live our life as the ego-self, oriented toward and dependent on the external world, as the acquired personality that we confuse with our real self. We think that we are our ego, our thoughts, beliefs, and patterns. We get raised to see ourselves as matter—the physical body that is separate from others; you versus me, competition rather than oneness. We identify with our age, gender, weight, ethnicity, job, or financial status—falsely assuming that these factors are what makes "us", while they are actually just illusory identifications to an artificial construct predominantly created by society. What we don't get taught, on the other hand, is that at the elementary core, we are indeed all the same. Our essence is none of the factors mentioned above. When we strip those away, all that is left is what we truly are: Pure consciousness and energy.

While we are born as "pure" creatures without an ego-identity, undisturbed by identification and thought patterns, we usually unlearn this way of living over the decades to come. We follow the accepted norms and let our ego determine how we act, think, and feel. Until we reach the point where we have enough and start longing for more. Each one of us must go our own way to rediscover who or what we truly are; there is no "one size fits all" approach for this (yet). For this, we must temporarily leave rationality, logic, and numbers behind and switch to feeling, trust, and intuition instead. We have to face our darkest shadows and fears to come out into the light at the end of the tunnel, accepting and integrating our new para-

Introduction

digms. The journey is not always an easy one, but it will eventually be worth it; the only way out of fear is through the fear.

We then understand that we are the creators of our own future—that everything is possible. Our own thoughts and emotions play a significant role in how we create and perceive reality. We are more powerful than we think we are, but we have to (re)learn to go beyond our physical bodies, not limited by space and time. Energy and frequency help us to communicate on a level beyond the perceptible, constantly shaping the life we (want to) live. We undeniably live in changing times, with people around the world waking up, longing for something else, something more meaningful and powerful, outside of our traditional way of life. The exact same thing also happened to me.

Until my early thirties, I had been a somewhat regular guy. I worked in finance in Frankfurt, Germany, had a girlfriend, and went on with my life without any big issues. I was completely happy in my situation for many years, until one day, the routine of working for long hours and practically only living for the weekends wasn't enough any longer. I felt an urge to escape the ever-repeating daily patterns of life. I wanted to explore what else was out there in the world. I needed to break free from all the responsibility and conventions that had dictated my whole life to that point. Immediately quitting my job was a step too far for me; I was not ready for it yet. I had to slowly approach what was eventually unavoidable, taking one step at a time. I moved from Frankfurt to London, still employed by the same company. Then I moved to New York, still with the same company. And then it finally happened: I

Introduction

could no longer ignore the screams from inside me. I had to face my fears and quit! What followed was two years of world travel, significant personal transformation, and rediscovery of what I truly am (what we all are) at the core. A journey full of fears, doubts, and uncertainties, which ultimately made me grow, learn to love, and trust in life. My quest for money, quest for purpose, and quest for love led me to my new guiding principle in life, which I had previously lost: I am supporting people in need around the world, spiritually as well as financially. With this book, I hope to lay the foundation to achieve exactly that.

It is a very personal piece containing many examples of my life from the past two years. Some are rather unpleasant and certainly nothing I would typically share in public. Could I transport the same depth or message without being appropriately detailed and honest along the way, though? Probably not. You are welcome to explore my vulnerable and imperfect side from all angles as long as it has the intended effects. This book will serve multiple target groups: Those seeking knowledge and ideas about topics still mostly classified as "spirituality" or "esoteric", although these have become much more scientifically substantiated over the last decade. We now know, for example, that at the fundamental level, we are all the same in the form of consciousness and energy. In addition, seasoned readers of novels and non-scientific books may find my story rather interesting, and hence, I would love to take them on the journey with me. Many things, both ups and downs, happened during that time, and consequently, there is a lot to learn—from my mistakes as well as from my insights. Lastly,

Introduction

anybody looking for travel entertainment or who is keen to examine the evolving psyche of an average guy in his early thirties is most welcome to take a seat and get their evaluation sheets out. You will get full access to all details. In all honesty, this book is intended to take you—the reader—along the path with me; to see what I see, to feel what I feel, to grow with me. I learned and changed a lot over those years and hope to relay some of the wisdom in my real-life examples.

Furthermore, this book has another unique angle to it—to my knowledge, nothing comparable has ever been done before. I have decided to pledge a portion of the sales proceeds for donations and charitable purposes, in line with my newly defined guiding principle in life. As I want to involve the readers of my book also beyond the actual story of the last two years, I will let each one of you vote on which specific projects we will donate to and help to implement in the future. There is no reason why I should decide this myself—we are all part of this enterprise now. The book contains a QR code and passcode with which you will have access to vote on the website: www.two-years.com. I am still amazed by this beautiful flywheel construct and sincerely hope that we, as a collective, will have the chance to help as many people as possible: The more books sell, the more people will find spiritual support, and furthermore, the more money will be available for financial support of people in need. Welcome to a new era of print utility and governance.

Introduction

Scan QR code to open the voting site

Enter passcode to access the site
Mt34cR21Si69

Life in Society

The first few paragraphs of this chapter will serve as an introduction to me, the author. I will crisply summarize the time between studying at university to employment a few years later in order to provide you with a sense of "status quo" from where the events begin to take place. You will find the first few chapters less detailed compared to the remaining ones, where my actual journey and transformation took place.

I got my B.Sc. in Business Administration in Germany, then did a gap year during which I spent six months as an intern in India, and afterward got my M.Sc. in Finance in the Netherlands. After I graduated from university, I immediately started working in investment banking in Germany, with the same company I interned with a year earlier in Mumbai, India. At that point, my life basically consisted of only two things: Work and pleasure. I was essentially just functioning as a robot, but I was fine with that. I was super excited by the work and enjoyed the thrill, challenge, and prestige of it. The late nights, multiple simultaneous projects, and tight deadlines were not easy at times, but that didn't bother me too much. I felt at home at my workplace—it gave me structure, probably a sense of purpose, and many colleagues who also became friends.

To that point, I had never asked myself any deeper questions about life because it never appeared necessary. I had a clear path in front of me; I was excited by the career game and my ego-driven ambitions to succeed, to be the best. I would say most young adults around my age still play along the traditional path that society suggests we follow, though I think a shift is taking place, and people are starting to ask questions of meaning and purpose at earlier ages—in the long run, this is probably a good thing. However, in the end, everybody has to go their own way and have certain experiences in a certain order to eventually reach their decision point to ask: Is this all there is?

If I had to describe the "me" from back then, I would summarize as follows: A boy in his mid-twenties (yes, still a boy) who perfectly functioned as an adult in the work environment. I could take on a lot of responsibility, drive projects independently, and handle colleagues as well as clients in a professional manner. But within, I was partially still a kid full of fears, uncertainties, and unhealed wounds, hence mainly defining myself via outside validation. It was what I had learned to do best over the years: Full focus on studying and working with the aim of having an important career, because that was what we all wanted to achieve or were illusioned to think we wanted. My personal development, on the other hand, was rather secondary. Hard to combine those two when you have a clear goal in front of you, isn't it? Especially with the latter being a potential complication for the former.

I was objectively functioning well in society and had achieved what we all mainly strive for in our first half of life. Good degrees, a well-paying and prestigious job, a girlfriend, and a stable group of friends. Subjectively, on the other hand, I had developed many addictive behaviors over the years, which took me some time to identify and address. My underlying main addiction was, and sometimes still is, dopamine. The tiny, seemingly harmless, yet so strong and powerful neurotransmitter that brings us pleasure and reward. Dopamine is part of our internal reward system, which, from the standpoint of evolution, is designed to reward us when we are doing things necessary for survival, e.g., eating, drinking, or reproducing. Our brains are hard-wired to seek those behaviors that release the most dopamine into our system. We then feel good, and naturally, we want more of that feeling. Nowadays, we often abuse—or rather, get abused—by our own reward system by overstimulating it with all sorts of addictive behaviors and substances.

So, how exactly did that addiction look in my daily life? First off, I smoked at least ten cigarettes a day and much more on the weekends when out with friends. I am sure every smoker or ex-smoker can relate very well to that. Each cigarette (or its nicotine) increases your dopamine base level by almost two times, thereby pleasing the mind in its daily, never-ending quest for the easiest way to reward and feel good—dopamine practically trains the brain to repeat the action. Second, I was addicted to stress. The adrenaline rush of solving one or multiple high-intensity tasks under time pressure and the subsequent feeling of relief once the task had been completed. Here, the dopamine release basically consists of two things: One, the reward of solving the challenging task, and two, being temporarily stress-free once the task has been completed —basically a reward in the form of pain avoidance. Third, I (or rather my ego-self) was addicted to outside validation, which in many cases is rooted in childhood. When the little boy or girl wants mommy's and daddy's love or attention and does almost anything to please them. Does that ring a bell? For example, when you came home from school and got good grades to present, you were the favorite child and got all the attention and love you wanted. But if the grades were not as expected, all of a sudden, that picture may have looked quite different. You were implicitly taught that your worthiness is determined by external factors. This early-adopted pattern often lasts until adulthood or even until death for some people, and that's why we all try to give our best and get as much confirmation from the outside as possible. We satisfy our ego-self with the illusion of worth being determined by external factors that oftentimes do nothing else but trigger a dopamine release. Finally, if I am honest with myself, I was probably also addicted to alcohol in one form or the other. Even though I did not drink during the week, I partied and drank a lot on the weekends. One, two, or three drinks and then going home was not my thing—it usually ended being a rather long night, with me drunk then hungover the next day. It was a habit I had developed in my teens and consequently was not so easy to break, as it conveniently helped me to take my mind off work and to fill the occasional void of "nothingness" (maybe a lack of purpose). Cheap dopamine release by alcohol consumption and other distractions is always preferable over becoming still, looking inside, and facing the truth, right?

To summarize, many addictions boil down to an underlying need to feel good/avoid pain and gain rewards in the form of dopamine release, even though it may not be obvious at first glance. Without the daily dose of our favorite neurotransmitter, we feel empty, lethargic, anxious, or simply not good. We need it. We want it. As much as possible. And all of our society is hooked on it. Unfortunately, mostly without even realizing it. Welcome to the dopamine nation![1]

I was basically living the "dull" life of work and pleasure for many years. Of course, I also took the typical vacation twice a year, flying somewhere sunny at the beach and taking my mind a bit off the usual environment and problems. However, slowly but steadily, something crept up inside me that screamed, "You want more free time. There is more to explore in this world than just this small, repetitive cosmos you have been operating in for years now." Please note that I am not implying our standard way of life is bad or inferior in any way. It just was not enough for me, personally, any longer at that point in time. Life was passing at lightspeed right in front of my eyes, but all I had been doing for years was work, sleep, pleasure, repeat. On the weekends, I would start reading a few books and stories about people who quit their jobs, traveled the world, tried something completely new, or at least took a sabbatical year. With each additional story I read, the desire to break free from this known and predictable environment became more frequent and intense. I could no longer deny it or lie to myself; something had to change. One of the main factors was the satisfaction from my work not being the same as it used to be: While I had loved the transaction-driven nature of it in the past, I slowly realized that it no longer satisfied me enough to dedicate all my time and energy to it. In the end, I wanted to feel alive; I wanted to feel good about the work I did. However, my passion and sense of purpose gradually diminished while my competence increased. Needless to say, a combination like that is not sustainable—the links in my Formula for Success were broken. In general, if any one of these components is no longer a given, we should start thinking about reasons and solutions:

Passion + Competence + Purpose = Formula for Success

Also, Frankfurt had become a pretty familiar environment by that time, with the same people always around, the same places to go, and the same things to do—it was definitely time for a change. The issue was that I had no idea what I wanted to do instead, work-wise, and I was way too afraid to just quit without a plan. The ego-self likes control and hates unpredictability or uncertainty, so it will give its all to make sure we are not doing anything out of the ordinary. In general, this is not necessarily a bad thing; the mechanism stems from evolution, and it's here to protect us to a certain extent (uncertainty = danger, hence our instinctive survival/fight-or-flight mode is activated), but at the same time, it also limits us drastically in pursuing our true passions or reaching our full potential, if we let it.

So, what to do? One of my colleagues suggested that I could do a one-year rotation in London in order to get into a different setting, learn something new, and network with more people within the company. At first, I hesitated because I didn't like all the uncertainty coming with it; I am sure most of us don't really like too much change and rather prefer to stay in a somewhat known, comfortable place. Nevertheless, after a few weeks of thinking time, I decided that it was the best thing to do as the new department would give me ideal complementary skills that I could use in my field of expertise. I initiated the process, and a few months later, I was finally able to rotate to London—by now I was simply excited, no more sign of fears and doubts. My girlfriend at that time fully supported my move, and we were confident that we could make this work; London was only one flight hour away from Frankfurt, and it was (supposed to be) for just one year. Back then, I didn't and couldn't have realized that this move to London was just me buying time, or to put it differently, me making my first step toward the final decision that would follow a few years later, to eventually quit. Though at that time, I was neither self-aware nor emotional enough to really feel what was actually going on inside me. But it didn't matter much because I had an exciting new chapter in front of me without having to leave the company and my familiar career in finance.

The year in London was indeed great. I learned a lot, really liked the team, and loved the city. My girlfriend came to visit every few weeks (or I visited her), and we became even closer during that time, despite the distance. The anticipation of finally seeing each other again and then indeed being together was, each time, a beautiful liaison. While we usually needed an hour or two to "get used to each other" again after several weeks without personal contact, it wasn't a big issue at all. We managed perfectly fine. She was happy, I was happy. It all seemed to work well; hence time was flying rather fast. The end of my one-year rotation approached, and I was confronted with the same question as the year before: What now? Staying in London would have definitely been an option, and the team also asked me to, but I knew that I didn't want to work in that specific field in the long run. The add-on knowledge I gained over the year was perfect in terms of depth and applicability, but nothing that would excite me "forever". At the same time, I felt it was not the right move to directly return to Frankfurt. The thought of having to go back to the same routine, environment, and workload made me feel somewhat uneasy. I had just begun to explore a tiny bit of whatever else was out there, and now I should go straight back to where I had initially started? It just didn't feel right. Even though back then I couldn't work with my intuition as clearly as I can today, it was already guiding me to a certain extent. This inner feeling and trust that neither of those two options was the right one was what made me look further.

I spent around two weeks thinking and lying awake in bed at night. I could flip and turn those two options around as much as I wanted, from all possible angles; it didn't change the fact that something inside me revolted against both. How about I take a break from work and travel for a while? Where would I go and what did I want to see? Did I even want that now? After a while, I also ruled out quitting at that stage, as I still felt motivated to learn more. I wasn't burned out or anything like that; it was something else that I was seeking. How about I change companies? Would that really help with anything? What would I want to do instead of banking? No surprise, exactly the same questions I had faced the previous year. And I had no answer to them, yet again. I simply didn't know.

Then, one day, I got the right inspiration. We had just worked on a cross-border project together with our US team, and I got along with them really well. I had built a reputable connection over the course of the project and could at least informally inquire about their team setup, deal flow, and culture. I talked with colleagues of all ranks, junior to senior, thoroughly forming my view. It was indeed a great fit, and I saw the opportunity emerging right in front of my eyes. There it was. I finally had a plan: I should try to move to New York within the company—if not now, then when? This was the perfect chance to acquire additional skills for my role once again, meet and network with new people, and live in the most exciting city in the world. By now, I almost felt a "routine" in changing departments within the company. I initiated the process, and a few weeks later, I received confirmation that I could move to New York City, with a minimum tenure of eighteen months. Even though NYC was obviously quite far away, and I barely knew any people there, I felt more relief and excitement than fear or doubt. After all, I had just bought another one and a half years of time before I would have to face the unavoidable question of my life again—I could worry about it later. Of course!

Next, I had to tell my girlfriend about my plans. I kept the whole thing to myself until I had the definitive confirmation—that was how I had always operated. I wanted to tell her in person the next time we met, as this was a rather big move and certainly also a challenge for our relationship. At that time, I was rather egoistic and self-centered when it came to career progression—the job had always been my priority, and personal relationships came after. She was obviously surprised and somewhat shocked when I finally let her in on my next move, but again, she supported me because she wanted to see me happy and fulfilled. She had a very good heart. I should also mention that I approached relationships quite differently back then; I didn't expect a "partner forever" but rather a partner for a period of time, depending on how things would develop. I wasn't even ready to make long-term plans for myself, so how could I do it for two people? I always had such a feeling of potentially missing out on something, that I was not yet ready to settle forever—even though I couldn't specifically pin it down, something in me knew that I had to follow another path or detour. Full flexibility is something we might not get to experience again later in life. Is it worth more, equal, or less than love, though? I don't know and wouldn't dare to judge, but at that time, the international career possibilities were more appealing than locking myself in for a potential long-term relationship that I wasn't actually ready for.

Two Years

The first few months in New York were great—I really liked the team, learned a lot, and most definitely partied a lot in that big concrete jungle. In a nutshell, life was essentially the same as it was in Frankfurt and London, mainly consisting of work and pleasure, just a tad more exciting based on the magic of NYC itself. My girlfriend wanted to visit me in March 2020 for the first time since I had left; however, out of nowhere, the great unknown variable Covid-19 entered the game. Three days before her planned flight to New York, the president put a travel ban for most European countries in place. Thus, our plans were shattered for the foreseeable future. We tried to keep our relationship alive via technology, but the time zone difference and general coronavirus-related mood swings didn't particularly help with that. Step by step, we drifted apart, physically by circumstance and emotionally by choice. She had her own struggles, and I had mine. Our messages and video calls became less frequent and our bond less tight.

From here on, things got very confusing, exciting, painful, and life-altering in a more or less sequential manner. I won't go into the details of how exactly the lockdown went down because we all have experienced it; I will just reiterate that our daily life structure and routine were suddenly ripped apart. Instead of going to work and interacting with people, we had to stay home and find comfort by ourselves. For me, the new home office was the badly lit apartment in Nolita, where I was living with two American roommates at the time. Both went home to their parents' houses, as did most of the American workforce, to avoid being potentially locked down in the city. NYC very quickly became a ghost town, something I had never seen before. Back then, I thought this would all be over in a couple of weeks and didn't panic or stress about it. Little did I know that things would remain in this awkward, ghost-like state for the remainder of my tenure. What timing to move to New York!

Breaking Out

Generally, I never had big issues with being alone and finding things to do myself; hence I made the best of the situation. On my work breaks, I took walks around the neighborhood, went to nearby parks to read books, and slowly extended my explorations to all areas of the city when work allowed for it. Ironically, a newly gained sense of freedom overcame me during those days of lockdown. I began to understand what it means to also have spare time during the week. The initial feeling of guilt for not being productive twenty-four-seven was gradually replaced with the excitement of further exploring the city. Yet, there was also a feeling of being trapped. Trapped at home, in one room, in front of a screen. Like in a cage. It was a state of in-betweenness with the option to go outside during the day whenever possible, while also being required to remain present for work. A weird mix of freedom and captivity. Something we all had to get used to.

We had formed a group of friends who worked hard during the week and distracted themselves with long and excessive house parties (obviously all clubs and bars were closed) on the weekends, basically continuing the dull work and pleasure cycle even during Covid. Fundamentally, nothing had changed. Only the circumstances were different. During that time, I also started cheating on my girlfriend. New York is a very sexual city, and almost everybody is looking for some fun, one way or the other. Of course, this doesn't justify any of my actions, but the explosive cocktail of physical and emotional distance, lockdown, and loneliness made me act in a way I never did before. While I was in London, I never even thought about cheating once. But things were different now. I was looking for company and comfort, as being alone in my apartment became pretty draining—after all, we are humans and need some form of social interaction, don't we? More and more, I distanced myself from my girlfriend, and I honestly also thought that she would never find out. "Once this all is over and back to normal in a few weeks or months, we will be able to see each other again and continue our relationship," I thought and added, "If things should stay in this weird state for longer, then I could not be constantly alone, anyway." I didn't like it and certainly didn't feel good about it, but I did what I (apparently) needed to do. The months passed by, and we each lived our own lives, she in Frankfurt, I in New York. We were still in contact, but quite honestly, it was nothing of substance.

Fast forward to September 2020. We decided to meet in Mexico, where the borders were open. And there the inevitable happened: She checked my phone and found out that I was cheating on her. Something neither she nor I would have ever imagined, as we had always had a trusting relationship in the past. Naturally, the remainder of the one-week vacation was rather awkward, and we consequently broke up. Now here I was, more or less alone in the big city, girlfriend gone, and sick of all the dull partying that had led me to this point. I realized that I had been a self-centered, egoistic, and probably also narcissistic idiot, not in control of his own yearnings. I felt sorry for what I did—she didn't deserve that. But I had done it, and I had to bear the consequences. I knew that I couldn't blame anything or anybody other than myself for what happened, but I decided that I had to part ways with my group of friends for the time being, as we all encouraged those questionable habits in each other. All of us were basically the same: Empty on the inside and looking to fill the void with meaningless pleasure in the form of parties and one-night stands. It was fun while it lasted, but I had to move on.

The timing was actually good (at least so I thought) for me, as I moved apartments upon my return to NYC. This time to a more spacious, light-filled apartment in the Financial District where I felt good, positive, and even indifferent to staying inside for most of the day. Here, I also learned that where and how we live indeed matters a lot. In that area, most people were "like me", and despite the streets being mostly empty and people being locked inside, there was still a comforting feeling of belonging and connectedness, with the people and the area in general. I didn't mind spending hours, days, and weeks inside, as I knew that the people in the building (mostly young and dynamic) faced the exact same issues, and we also occasionally met. A few months later I would learn what a big difference those factors can make—while here I had a pleasant experience of the upside, my next apartment would bring a rather unpleasant experience of the downside. We will come back to that point later.

Around the third to fourth quarter of 2020, most markets witnessed a strong, almost manic, run-up and acceleration of the bull cycle, to a large extent driven by retail investors locked up at home and looking for meaning and excitement in their physically limited lives. So did I. I spent quite a bit of time each day diving deeper into certain niches, playing around with some smaller amounts of money, and hitting the first big lucky shots. That's how markets tend to work after all, right? You get a few winnings in the beginning that delude you into thinking you are the world's greatest investor or trader, only to realize later that you actually don't know anything and simply got lucky. Of course, the same also happened to me. The weeks went by, I kept playing the game of working and doing some speculating on the side, made some good gains as well as chunky losses, but the initial enthusiasm slowly faded, as it didn't provide me with any deeper sense of meaning either—in most cases it simply boiled down to: "How many people can you convince to buy after you, so that you can sell your assets at an opportunistic maximum gain." Yes, there undeniably is huge excitement when you hit the first big wins. Nothing beats the dopamine rush you get from seeing your (virtual) money doing multiples within days, not even sex or drugs. But this euphoria is partially canceled out by the losses you take, and the whole process of up and down becomes very exhausting—especially when more money is on the table. If one has always fed their ego-identity based on external success factors, any bigger losses are perceived as failure and will probably rip sizable holes in such ego-identity and, consequently, in self-confidence.

I felt a sense of meaninglessness as well as a reemerging loneliness coming up inside me. It had been quite a while since I'd had any deeper human interaction besides some superficial small talk or video calls. However, at that time, I wasn't sensitive enough to realize what had happened to me over the months. I was so deep into my work and gamble routine that I had totally neglected social contacts. I hadn't even noticed how much time I spent alone. I was always busy, either in front of the computer or on my phone. My eyes were practically glued to the screens. My mind constantly rotating. Weeks of high intensity with few to no breaks. By now, the initial excitement of the paradoxical freedom in lockdown had settled. The missing human connection and sense of belonging made all these numbers on a screen appear rather meaningless. Without the typical office environment, the daily interaction in different project teams, and the shared energy of achieving the same goal, that isolated sitting in front of a computer screen—massaging numbers in Excel sheets—became pointless. Once again, I was just functioning as a robot. A lonely robot.

At the beginning of 2021, I had to move apartments again, as the lease for my current place ended. I could have stayed at that apartment for longer, but that would have required a renewal of the lease for another two years. This was a burden I did not want to take on at that point because I wanted the flexibility to leave NYC (my eighteen-month minimum tenure would end in May 2021) without any contractual issues. Hence, I started looking for a new place to stay for the remaining few months and found an option on the Lower East Side which I signed for a six-month term. I packed my two cartons of clothes and moved—without owning any furniture, this part was always easy.

A few days passed, and I started to notice the overall heavy and negative energy in the area and the building itself. It was still wintertime, everything was kind of gray and dark, and I felt totally disconnected and different from most people around there. Before, I used to live in areas where most people were young and like-minded, but in the new area and building, it was completely different. Some very old people, some very scared middle-aged people, and some seemingly depressed people, but no one who was "like me". I think this is where my old ego-identity started to slowly crumble over the following weeks; I lost my sense of stability, belonging, and identity. Many months of isolation with little to no illusory external validation of self-worth from colleagues and superiors at work, or otherwise, started to show their effect. I didn't feel part of anything any longer. No class, no group, no ethnicity. I had lost the defining foundations that made "me" through the years. I no longer was anyone. I was just a lonely person. The level of pain piling up inside me had reached a critical point.

The next situation I remember very vividly. An asset that I had sold off a few months ago for a good profit started to gain traction again after a while of sideways movement. It was late evening, and I was lying on the sofa watching a movie, occasionally checking my phone. I screened the few assets on my watchlist and suddenly noticed that particular one with significant low-time-frame momentum. I immediately ran to my computer to check the status and deep down knew that this was my time. This was my opportunity to get on board again, to simply buy and hold for the next few months. I was exhausted by all the volatility and screen time and simply wanted to remain in one position going forward, but the right moment hadn't emerged until that point. Now here it was. All I had to do was act. One more transaction, and then I would simply lie back and focus on work and private life. I had my hand on the mouse over the "buy" button, and all I had to do was click, just one click. Yet something inside me revolted. "Don't do it. It is too late already, anyway. The risk of losing it all is too high." And I didn't. Whatever was speaking from inside me convinced me not to click. I was too exhausted. I couldn't act with my typical routine and sharpness. Apparently, I was out of touch with the market.

Even today, I sometimes ask myself if this was indeed due to me being out of rhythm with the market, and my confidence being shattered due to a streak of losses in the weeks before, or whether the "real" me (the soul, not the ego) was crying out for a radical change in my life. I strongly believe it was the latter, as I have now realized that everything in life is guided, and there is no effect without a cause. Something deep inside me was asking for this event to happen so that I could eventually break free from everything. From work, from conventions, and from belief systems that kept me in a cage of limitations and fears. This moment was a decisive contributor for me to radically change my life a few months later.

Over the coming weeks, I watched that particular asset run up in an extremely parabolic manner, yet I was not capable of buying in—I had made my decision. I could no longer take that emotional rollercoaster of up and down, and hence all I could do was watch from the sidelines. Every day, I had to watch the asset increase in value. Even though I knew that it was pointless, I couldn't stop checking charts and numbers in every free minute I had. Quite honestly, I was pretty obsessed. Probably the most painful thing one can do is to calculate what one could have made in potential gains if one hadn't sold off the position in the past or at least had bought in again at a certain point. That is exactly what I did, thereby inflicting maximum pain on myself. I watched my former (now non-existent) position run up to eight figures at the peak.

It was a level of pain I never had to endure before. No physical pain I had ever experienced came even close to it. No past breakup was comparable in the slightest. I could no longer bear it and eventually broke down. I had barely slept, eaten, or thought straight during those days and was no longer functioning properly. I was completely drained and fatigued. While I had already been struggling with my crumbling ego-identity in the weeks before, this painful event was the final trigger. Everything came together at once: The sense of not belonging, the loneliness, the indecisiveness about my future, and finally, the self-inflicted pain from the markets. A heavy cocktail of fear, panic, and desperation that I had no chance to longer ignore. I had to feel right through it. And it was awfully hard.

Two Years

So hard that I had to partially repress my emotions with alcohol, something that I had never (consciously) done before. Drinking to cope—sadly, I had reached a new low. In that moment, it was my only tangible option, though. I knew it would get better over time.

In the following weeks I forced myself to stay away from the screens as much as possible, except for work. I tried to spend more time outside to balance out the physical and mental turmoil in me. Days flew. Time glided on. Tick tock. One day, I was sitting on a bench in the park next to my building and realized that I really needed to face the unavoidable question: What was I going to do with my life? My tenure in New York would end in two months, but I was so stuck in my routine and obsession with markets that I had completely neglected to think about the future. After more than a year of working from home, I felt totally disconnected from work and even from the world in general. Everything had lost its appeal. Nothing seemed important anymore. I needed a drastic change. What I needed most was freedom. Freedom from numbers that lost all meaning, freedom from daily Zoom meetings that felt surreal, freedom from all responsibility, and freedom from New York City—by now I had explored each part of the city multiple times and was honestly tired of the concrete jungle and its skyscrapers. Even though all teams (Frankfurt, London, and New York) called me regularly with offers to come back or stay, I simply couldn't do it. I needed to get out, into nature, and clear my mind.

This is the point where I ultimately had to face my fears and pull the trigger: To quit my job! A job that had been my ego-identity for all those years, that gave me a sense of purpose and meaning in life, that provided me with social stability and a good income. But the lockdown took all those advantages away, and all that was left was working from home, alone in a room. Nobody knew how long that situation would continue, and I was definitely not willing to find out. I needed to break free. What had piled up inside me for years—starting in Frankfurt, continuing in London, and ending in New York—could finally release. There was no more buying time, no more running from the decision; my time to act was now. The end of May 2021 was officially my last day at work. From here on, a period of major uncertainties but also endless possibilities lay ahead of me. A period spiked with quests that would make me learn, grow, and transcend. A period of: Two years.

Quest for Money

After being formally free, I stayed another few days in the city to pack my things and, more importantly, to decide where I wanted to go. My ability to think straight, smile, sleep, and eat slowly returned, and I felt a bit more grounded again. It felt as if a heavy burden had been taken off my shoulders; I had finally made my long-postponed decision and would only look forward from here. I could finally leave this dark and unpleasant area, building, and workroom behind and go straight into the sun. I swiftly decided that the best option to start my travel would be Florida, a state filled with palm trees and beaches. Until that point, I had never booked a one-way vacation ticket because most of us—including me—usually go for one or two weeks to a spot with an exact plan in hand for where and how to return. This was about to change with a new, unfamiliar, but exciting lifestyle of making no plans, being spontaneous, and going wherever and whenever I wanted. A clean cut from the seven years of "living for work" life model. The contrary and sunny environment excited me to do all sorts of activities that hadn't been possible in the months before. For example, I started an accelerated course in skydiving to be able to jump on my own, had a helicopter ride over the coast, and went on sea explorations by boat, jet ski, and kayak. All these adrenaline-rich activities in nature I surely needed after being trapped in the same place for the whole last year—it was a total relief, and I finally started feeling good again, could laugh again, and could just sit down and relax. Something that I was previously afraid of having lost forever.

In Key West, Florida, I also had my first encounter with the topics of mindfulness, meditation, and spirituality in general. I walked along the streets and saw a tarot reader sitting at her small pop-up desk, offering her services. I thought to myself, "Why not?! You have never done it before. Let's see what comes out of it—you are here to have new experiences, after all." I went over to her, asked for a reading, paid her, and we began. She laid the cards down for me and went over a few key topics—interestingly, most of the aspects matched my situation quite accurately. I will not opine on the validity of such readings here as the key point is not the method itself, but that the experience was the first door opener for me into a world I would have laughed at a few months prior. After the reading was over, she gave me a list of a few guided meditations that she suggested I should follow daily. At this point, I had no relation to these topics at all but decided to give it a try regardless—I had nothing to lose but potentially a lot to gain; that was promising enough! To be frank, it took me a few days to really get started as my left-brain-focused, rational, and logical belief system simply wasn't trained to accept those mystic things as real. However, eventually I conceded, and over the following days, I would sit down at the shore and do the meditation homework. It was okayish. Given these were my first few times trying any of this, I did not feel or experience much. Nevertheless, after each time, there was at least a slight sense of relaxation and calmness. It was a start. It was also a form of confirmation for me—that my decision to quit was the right one and that I needed to trust what was to come. Those days were my first encounters with anything spiritual, but I would not get back to it until almost a year later.

I continued my trip through Texas, Arizona, and California. My travel style during this time was still the same: Seeking new experiences, eating good food, and meeting new people along the way. Simply enjoying whatever I did, wherever I was, without any schedules. At that point, there was no need or desire to dive much deeper into topics around self-development or spirituality; what was important was that I gave myself permission to enjoy the newly won freedom without guilt or regrets. While the old me was afraid to spend larger amounts of money on anything (habits coming mainly from parents and grandparents who grew up at a time when money was always a scarce resource), I promised myself not to count every dollar during the trip. I deserved to spend it on myself after the last seven years of hard work. It was not an easy habit to break though, especially after having just experienced that severe pain and sensation of lack and loss in the prior weeks.

Once I arrived in San Francisco, I partook in an organized tour with a small group of eight people to Yosemite National Park.

I really liked that place—diverse in nature and full of hiking trails. Here I met the woman I'll call J; she and her friend were in the same group, and they were traveling through the US together. We came into contact and spent some time together on walks over the next two days in the park. As it turned out, the two had roughly the same travel route ahead of them as me: California, Vegas, and then back to New York. We exchanged numbers and agreed to meet again in Vegas a few days later. There, J and I spent a few fun nights together and also talked about our respective stories, which turned out pretty similar: She worked long hours in the office for many years, saw life passing in front of her eyes, and hence decided to quit and travel more. When I told her about my story, she could clearly feel the pain inside me with regard to not wanting to go back to work anytime soon. She could empathize with me, as she had been in the exact same situation just a few months prior. Hence, she told me about the cloud storage business she was involved in on the side, basically earning her passive income and providing her the required freedom to travel. She didn't ask for money or anything like that but simply shared her "secret" to having enough time and resources for traveling. Naturally, my first thought was that it sounded like a total scam and certainly nothing I would want to get involved in, and thus we left it at that. Today, I understand that the crossing of our paths was not a coincidence; we were two people on the same frequency looking for the same thing: Freedom and travel. We had to have certain experiences together, learn together, and grow together in the months to follow. We would become companions for a time.

Two Years

After Vegas, I went back to New York, where my two months of travel through the US ended. My visa would expire in a few days, and I had to leave the country. J and her friend also came to NYC, and we met up again to spend a few days together. At that time, the city was almost back to normal compared to two months before. Bars and restaurants were properly open again, and people who had left the year before slowly began to return. For the first time since Covid started, I actually enjoyed the environment again. The city was not that dark, empty block of sadness any longer, but on its way back to the lively and diverse center of excitement that it used to be. My new perspective of being totally free also contributed to that, of course. I felt so much better, recharged, and optimistic after the two-month timeout traveling around the States. It was exactly what I needed. I don't even dare to think what would have happened if I had simply stayed where I was, and that's probably for the best. It was time to leave that chapter behind and look forward to the future.

The day of saying goodbye had come, and toward the end of July, I flew home to Germany—my confusing, exciting, painful, and life-altering time in the US was now over. I felt grateful for all my experiences, good and bad, as they had basically handed me the ticket to finally change and initiate a new chapter of my life, something that I had played around with in my mind for years. Here I would like to introduce an analogy that, from my perspective, illustrates the dilemma most of us are in quite well: Real change is not the caterpillar becoming more colorful, beautiful, or bigger. Real change is the caterpillar becoming the butterfly that it is destined to be.

By simply amending a few outside factors, we will likely not have the real transformation that we want and need—rather, a fundamental restructuring of our life models, patterns, and belief systems will help us to become who we want to be. Do you see how well this describes my situation, one I'm sure most of us share? I used to change job departments and locations from Germany to the UK and the US, and became a better caterpillar. However, only once I decided to take the final step of quitting my known environment, the one I felt so safe and secure in, did I pave the way for the real transformation that would later allow me to become the butterfly that I have always been destined to be.

Back home, I spent a few weeks with family in my hometown, as I hadn't seen them in person for almost two years. It felt good to be back in the comforting and peaceful environment where I grew up, surrounded by nature. I didn't tell anyone what exactly had happened during the last few months in NYC, as I preferred to keep such personal matters private. Everyone has their own ways of dealing with these situations, and mine was to process it myself. I didn't mind speaking with strangers that I met at restaurants or bars about it, as I would likely never see them again. Their judgments and opinions didn't matter to me. Family or close friends were something different, though. I didn't like to reveal those rather "secret" sides of myself—I would typically only share what I felt comfortable with. We all usually aim to show ourselves from the best, seemingly perfect side, don't we? So did I. I kept my façade up and continued my regular way.

Two Years

After a while at home, the initial bliss of being back settled. The familiar question of "What now?" emerged back to the surface. I knew that it was too early to go back to work, as I had just won my new freedom; also, I had no idea what I wanted to do in life and was not yet ready to think about it seriously. Hence, I parked the question for the time being and conveniently escaped to another known distraction. As I had not spent a single minute on markets over the last two months, I decided to give it another try to see if things would work more in my favor this time. Unfortunately, by now, the market environment had somewhat turned, and the easy "throwing darts" period was pretty much over. People around the world were getting back to work, lockdowns and restrictions were lifted, and most retail investors had probably gambled away their temporary gains to a large extent by now. Somehow, my mind still held on to the idea of money being able to show me a way out of the uncertainty and lack of direction in my life. I made a few more speculations that would later turn out not to be on my side either, but in that moment, I was not ready to give up hope, or rather attachment, yet. I still had that itching feeling in me that I needed to try it, that I could land another big shot comparable to that one asset that I sold too early and that I painfully watched going parabolic without me profiting from it.

In addition, spending time on markets at least kept me busy and involved during that time. I couldn't just cut off everything, it was a step too fast—that transformation would only happen months later. Staying engaged provided me with a temporary sense of (fake) purpose, i.e., I had at least something to work toward, even though I couldn't see or accept yet that it was nothing but an illusion. However, I needed to learn exactly that by experiencing it to the fullest myself. How else could you truly know, right? You could listen to what other people say and take it for granted, but will you then ever truly know that you are living your life in a way that is fully aligned with your own values and beliefs? For me, I always had to live through everything until I was done with it. I remember a few friends at university saying that I had no sense of moderation, and they were quite right. In my opinion, confusion (about oneself, society, and life in general) largely results from not following one's own feelings or ideas to their full depth, but rather backing away from them to conform to normality, or to put it differently, to avoid potential discomfort.

While most material things per se (first and foremost financial wealth) don't offer any deeper meaning or purpose, they provide us with the necessary means to pursue exactly those. Quite a paradoxical relationship deeply anchored in the modern world of capitalism. A game we unfortunately all have to play if we want to achieve a certain degree of freedom, safety, and stability for us and our loved ones. The tricky part is that we all need it—simply to survive. We need to take care of our families, provide shelter and food, secure education, and ideally save a little for occasional leisure activities. Personally, I never had to worry about those basic needs as I grew up in a safe and sound environment; for that I am very grateful. However, at the same time, I also acknowledge that a large part of the world population simply does not have and likely never will have the financial means to live carefree or to pursue their deepest dreams. While in the digital age it has become directionally easier for anyone to participate in and make use of the global capitalist system, the existing wealth gaps are unlikely to shrink but rather increase. For those readers interested in exploring the world with little financial resources, there are free alternatives available that basically allow for immersing anywhere on the planet—volunteering or work and travel. I tried that form of traveling in Norway myself and would highly recommend it to anyone seeking real and authentic experiences; I will circle back to it later.

After almost two months with family and friends in Germany, it was time to move on. I thought that I should do a three-month trip via train through selected countries in Europe and decided on Denmark, France, and Spain. I started my travels in Denmark, where I spent a few wonderful weeks in small towns in nature—I tried to avoid big cities whenever possible, as I felt rather caged by them at that time. In the past, I never had any issue with cities and genuinely liked them, but that sensation changed post-NYC. I had seen it all; bars, restaurants, clubs, and all other forms of entertainment that are usually offered to us unconscious slaves. What I had barely seen or experienced over the last few years, on the other hand, was nature. Calmness. Relaxation. Silence. No stress. No competition. No hustle. I was not looking for adrenaline-rich activities so much anymore, but rather simply being in nature and reconnecting to myself. I took long daily walks, explored the surroundings, and allowed myself to continue enjoying the simple things of life without feeling any regrets.

While traveling, I also kept in touch with J. We would text or talk from time to time and keep each other updated on what we were doing and where we went. Nothing super intimate, but also nothing totally distant—something in between. One day we talked and decided that she would join me on the train trip for the remaining two months. A week later, we met in France. We picked some magnificent locations, such as Mont Blanc, Colmar, and Annecy (to name a few), and really had a great time together. We were basically travel companions who were sharing the same temporary destination: The world. While having all these exciting experiences together, we also talked again about the cloud storage business that J was involved in. Since we met in the US, I had gotten to know her much better and felt that I could trust her, thus opening myself to this opportunity. We talked about the mechanics, went through the calculations together, and discussed a path forward for me to join. A few weeks later I went in with a sizable amount, as I had not yet given up the dream of being free forever and escaping the entrenched office environment that I was not ready to go back to. The idea of money potentially solving all my problems was still persistent.

Everything went well for a while, and we enjoyed our trip to the fullest, staying at majestic locations in nature, eating really good food, and having a few occasional drinks in the evenings. It felt as if it was the weekend every day of the week. It swiftly became the standard. The rented houses, the daily new restaurants, and the general weekend mood weren't that exciting any longer—the contrast was missing. It became harder to appreciate those things when we had them at our disposal wherever and whenever we wanted. Overindulgence in these basic pleasures slowly lost its initial appeal. We kept going like this for some time, though—why change something that brings you the desired daily pleasure dose, right? Referring to the chapter Life in Society of this book, you will see that at this point I had simply replaced some of the old dopamine sources that were connected to work with new ones that were related to the pleasures of travel. Technically, nothing had changed yet. If anything, I had temporarily added a few more items to the list.

Next, we crossed the border to Spain, where we spent a few weeks in selected calm towns along the coast. However, things started to get shaky here with regard to our cloud storage investment: A temporary payout restriction was put in place by the operators, people started to get nervous, and some form of "bank run" happened—the literal textbook sequence of events. I have seen this pattern over and over again throughout the years, in all sorts of markets, including equities and unregulated assets; it always ends the same way. What made me so angry here was the timing. I had just come in two months ago, and this thing had to collapse exactly now? Why not a bit earlier? Was it just a Ponzi scheme after all? Why me? Looking back on it today, I realize things usually happen the way they have to happen, but back then, this was very hard to accept. Of course, I was tempted to blame J for all of this, and my ego started constructing stories about how all this was made up to rip me off. However, I confirmed via multiple ways that she had nothing to do with it. She lost her money the same way I did. And this is where I learned one of many lessons I would encounter over the next months: Forgiveness.

We continued to travel in Spain together, and every day I started anew to practice patience, acceptance, and trust, all in order to be able to forgive her and myself for what had happened. I knew there was no one else to blame but myself, but aren't we always trying to make other people or circumstances responsible for our own bad decisions? Yes, we do. All the time. The old me would have probably cut her off immediately, taking the pain inside and looking for excuses everywhere else; the new me, that I had slowly started to transform into, luckily took the other approach. I did not let my ego control this situation—a first positive sign of personal growth away from the self-centered guy that I used to be. I didn't want to let all my anger, pain, and frustration out on her; that was the wrong way. I needed to deal with these emotions myself. I had to be able to be with and around her every day, knowing that "because of her" I had just lost a significant amount of money. Looking her in the eyes without negatively judging her. It certainly wasn't an easy task, but I managed to stick with it. We finished our trip together mostly in peace; J flew back home, and I made my way back to Germany for a few weeks to digest what had happened. I didn't really want to believe it. I had lost another big chunk of money. That couldn't be real. I thought about it from all angles but ultimately let go of it. There wasn't anything I could do. It happened, it was my own fault, and I had to accept it. Quite honestly, after the maximum pain I had dealt with in NYC, this loss couldn't even bother me that much anymore. Somehow, I was less attached to it. It strengthened my resilience.

As a consequence of these events, I spent quite a while thinking about the general dynamic of markets and related Ponzi scheme characteristics. What we usually think about when hearing the term is a scheme that has no intrinsic value, in which later investors are paying out earlier investors, i.e., the system will collapse when the payout is greater than the pay-in, or to put it differently, when supply is greater than demand. With that in mind, isn't everything in life in some form a variation of such a scheme? Let us consider some selected examples below and decide together.

First, the global stock market is probably the most fitting example: Early investors are paid off (selling for profit) by later investors coming in and driving the stock price up, i.e., demand is greater than supply. However, if this dynamic turns and no one else buys in, the stock would either stay stable (assuming it pays a dividend) or would trend toward zero if those early investors look for more profitable alternatives elsewhere; then supply would be greater than demand, and the stock would collapse unless a new equilibrium is reached.

Or consider any product in the services industry (lawyer, consultant, etc.): If there are not enough clients who are interested in such services and thereby support the continuation of the business, then supply exceeds demand, and the service provider will eventually be forced to discontinue. Thus, continuation of services for the existing client base (=payout) depends on new prospective clients joining in (=pay-in); in that sense, later customers are paying out earlier customers. Otherwise, the system would collapse.

In the most extreme case, consider life itself: If people stopped having newborns (=demand) and there was no younger generation supporting the existence of humanity on this planet (=supply), our society as we know it today would collapse, i.e., supply would exceed demand. Pension schemes would no longer work, companies would have to shut down, and eventually the whole economy would break and the human species would completely vanish. Our existence is fundamentally based on such a construct.

I do not want to go deeper into this excursion, but I wanted to provide some food for thought for the interested reader. We are facing all conceivable varieties of Ponzi-like structures in our daily life but often don't perceive them as such simply because "it has always been done like that." While there is a clear distinction vis-a-vis an artificially created scheme with the intention to defraud and an actual ecosystem with a real product, the underlying supply and demand dynamics are largely the same. No society, system, or product/service can sustainably survive without sufficient demand; it would collapse. With that in mind, the world can be seen from a completely different angle, and certain things may become easier to accept and adapt to. Nothing has value, or anything can be valuable. Whatever the free market decides. Wherever the demand goes.

It was October by now, but I was still not yet ready to face any concrete thoughts of going back to work. It had been "only" half a year since I quit my job and there was so much more to explore, and honestly, I still did not know what I wanted to do with my life. When I look back to that time, I sometimes ask myself if my unwillingness to simply go back to work came from pure ignorance or if it was, rather, the higher guidance already at work without me noticing it, telling me to trust the process and go my way without a specific plan for a bit longer. I am mostly convinced it is the latter, as today I realize how everything, each event, each interaction, and each loss, was related and had to happen exactly the way it happened. Still, occasionally the doubting thoughts of my ego-self come through, trying to explain those events from a rational perspective of coping strategies. Maybe it was a mix of both.

I wanted to go somewhere warm that was not too far away from home, and I decided on Greece. I booked an apartment in a small town on the coast and spent the following three weeks there. It was a great environment to go for runs and long bike rides to temporarily clear my mind of all the negative (over)thinking. I was still attached to the idea of needing to make it all back despite having lost so much, i.e., my ego-mind was still hurt and not yet ready to let go of all that had happened. However, I had basically speculated all I had away by now and didn't have any resources left to "play around" further. I was fully invested. All I could do was wait and hope that one of the remaining speculations would somehow take off. But it didn't look good. The market was saturated. Not many players left. I had to accept that there was no more room to maneuver for me. And that was good! As I could no longer participate in the market, it was easier to gradually let go, to detach from the situation. I would still follow its developments, but I wasn't obsessed with it any longer. An important first step in the right direction.

One evening the audiobook of Paulo Coelho's *The Alchemist* popped up in my suggestions, and I remembered that I had read the print version a few years ago. It had given me a lot of strength and hope at that time—the months before I decided to leave Frankfurt for London. I immediately knew that I had to consume it again. It was so helpful back then; surely it would also help me this time around. For the first time in weeks, I was able to control my thoughts, shut down my mind, and become present in the moment. Just the audiobook and me. Each piece of wisdom transmitted between the lines reminded me to never lose hope, to trust that sometimes certain, seemingly negative, events must happen, only to lead us to the actual treasure we are destined to find in our life. The journey is one of many ups and downs: Without bad, there is no good; without old, there is no new; without darkness, there is no light. Life is contrast; always changing. It was exactly what I needed to hear in that moment. I finally found new hope again. Maybe I had to lose all that money. Maybe it was all part of a bigger plan that I could not yet understand. Maybe I was Santiago. With my regained confidence, I started to think about the next destination. Some Asian countries started reopening their borders for tourists without the need for a multiple-week quarantine; thus, J and I decided to travel through Thailand together. Our time was not up yet.

We visited some of the most stunning places, including beaches, mountains, and rural villages—a simple way of life on the scooter. Something came to my mind while taking a long ride through the rural towns, with nothing but the wind from the ride and the beautiful scenery around me: The less I possess, the more flexible I am—and spinning it one step further—the more flexible I am, the fewer limitations I have. The materialistic world (in the sense of physical products) had never provided me with any deeper sense of fulfillment; rather, it trapped me in a fixed environment that made me feel imprisoned. What I needed was freedom and flexibility! Flexibility to do whatever I want, to have new experiences where and when I want, and to meet new people from all "layers" of society around the world. In addition, I needed to understand myself better, needed to think, needed to feel, and needed to heal. Although I did not specifically focus on improving or healing myself back then, the urge slowly made its way up from deep inside me, a feeling that I could no longer deny. After a cozy New Year event in the Chiang Mai mountains, I flew back home to spend some time with my family again. My dad had been diagnosed with an advanced stage of cancer the year before, and nobody knew with certainty how long he would have left. Our working assumption at that time was "up to a few years", so we always made sure to spend enough time together.

During the days at home, I would again take long walks and think about life in general, wondering if there was more to it than what I had experienced so far. Don't get me wrong, it was wonderful to have all this new free time to travel around the world and soak in all these unique impressions. However, this could not be "it" for the rest of my life, could it? It was February 2022 by now, and I felt that something needed to change—I was longing for something else. It wasn't going back to work, it wasn't more or different food, it wasn't anything from the external, materialistic world at all. It was something else, and I was about to find out what.

The following scene was certainly a key moment that paved the way for my remaining travels. One evening I was sitting in the living room with my mom, and we talked about my situation and how I felt about it. I had realized a sense of exhaustion from the "pleasure travel" was coming up inside me over the last weeks, and it seemed that I was ready to take the next step. I noted, "I have now eaten all the good food, seen many beautiful places, and experienced a lot of new things. But what is next?" She didn't make any immediate remarks about my statement, but we talked a little bit around it and then watched some television together. The next day she placed a small piece of paper on the desk on the table in the living room, which stated, "By now, you have achieved all that the outside world has to offer. It is now time to look inside." At first, I didn't like that she would try to influence my life in this way—few would really like that in their thirties, right? But it was the right hint at exactly the right time. I was ready to pick up again on the concepts of mindfulness and spirituality that I had dipped my toes in around eight months earlier in Key West, Florida. We did not talk further about that piece of paper because, after all, everybody must go their own way to rediscover who or what they truly are—there is unfortunately no "one fits all" approach for it (yet). I silently accepted her invitation to look inside.

My quest for money, which I naively thought could solve all the big unknowns and provide direction in life, basically just ended in me taking some significant cumulative losses in the mid-six figures. At this point, there was nothing else to do but let go: Of my ego-identity, of old belief systems, and of illusory control. I had to accept what was and find happiness in each moment instead of short-term dopamine pleasure traps driven by external factors. My quest for purpose began.

Quest for Purpose

Over the next few days, I would indeed start diving into the topics of "alternative" views on life and the world (e.g., the power inside us, being conscious and mindful, meditation as a tool, etc.) by listening to podcasts and recordings online. In the beginning it was all a bit blurry, and I couldn't make much of it yet, given I was still the same, rational guy operating primarily with his left-brain side responsible for analytical, methodical, and fact-based thinking. To that point, I had probably rarely used my right-brain side except on a few select occasions—feeling, imagination, and intuition were not of much use for "working robots", after all.

I continued with my long nature walks around our hometown while listening to more and more of those recordings. Each time, a little bit of wisdom would stick with me. Some statements simply gave me comfort in having done the right thing, some opened me up to a more relaxed and less stringent approach to life, and some simply sounded attractive but still would somewhat interfere with my narrow belief system. Something kept me going down this path, as I felt there must be more to it than just the words and nice talking that it sometimes appeared to be; my persistence would turn out to be a good decision for the year ahead.

At that time, I also started journaling, of course rather roughly in the beginning, noting down those new concepts as well as my thoughts and feelings. The magical, handmade notebook covered in leather that I had bought a few months earlier in Sedona, Arizona, finally found its first occasion of use after a long idle period. The act of writing helped me to organize and digest all the new information. My brain would, step by step, start to recognize the material not only as immaterial one-off things that we face countless times throughout the day, but also as repeating established facts that help to restructure the mind on its way to accepting new paradigms. For someone like me, who had been dealing with numbers and logic for most of his life, such a material shift in views and beliefs would definitely take time. I was used to having tight plans, not leaving anything to chance; working hard, always being busy; and following my ego-self wherever it wanted to take me. And now I should simply give up all these decade-old patterns and believe there is something more fundamental going on inside us? Something that no one ever taught us about in school? That none of my friends or colleagues had ever talked about before? No, it wasn't that easy. I had to be convinced. I needed more and different sources to form my view. But I had to be honest, it felt good and exciting to learn something new. It would be a lengthy process, and I was just at the very beginning.

I also noted down a first-trial version of what I thought I wanted in life. That later turned out not to be the things that I truly wanted long-term, but at least I tried and made a step forward. It is also questionable whether we can ever truly know what we want—don't we always get somewhat bored after a while and seek the next exciting thing to do? Whether it be a new job, a new city or country to live in, a new hobby, or even starting a family. Only to realize a while later that the feeling of "something missing" is slowly creeping back. There exist a variety of views and theories on this specific aspect, and it also partially depends on each individual person's character, but I think we can agree on the bottom line that a final steady state in life is something rather illusory. Life means change. We never stand still. If not our minds, then for sure our bodies will do their part. Our cells are constantly changing, replacing, and renewing themselves. It takes around a decade for all cells in our bodies to be completely replaced, and the cycle repeats as long as we live. How could we then ever be "the same" as we used to be? Right, we can't. Not our bodies and not our minds. Imagine still having the same intellect, hobbies, or desires that you had as a teenager. Surely that wouldn't feel right.

During these days at home, I hadn't specifically picked up on meditation again. Until one day, when I returned from my walk and had the first of many insightful moments. It was a beautiful walk, and I felt very energized, having just understood a new concept that I had tried to wrap my head around in the days before. I deserved to rest for a bit and sat down in the comfortable living room chair, letting my mind wander. After a while, I lay back; surprisingly, all thinking had stopped by now, and I put my full attention on my individual body parts, one after the other. I had never really attempted to do this on purpose in the past and also wasn't sure if it was some form of meditation or relaxation that more experienced people would usually do, yet it simply came to me intuitively. Starting from the top, I let the attention flow around each part of my head—the forehead and hairline, the right and left side of the eyes where the first wrinkles usually show up, down the cheeks, and finally to the mouth. I put my attention on the gums and went around the teeth, feeling each individual one—and I actually felt them. That was a completely new sensation for me, at least consciously practicing it. I felt a very warm and comforting feeling of relaxation after this half-hour exercise and apparently got a glimpse of what it is like to master the mind, shut down repetitive thoughts, and feel the essence of what is really left after taking those things away: Pure awareness.

Naturally, no beginner can sustain such states for a prolonged period, and consequently, I fell back into my typical inner restlessness and thinking patterns thereafter. That is how the process works though; one gets beautiful breadcrumbs of experiences from time to time, but the effort to have them repeatedly and sustain them longer lies within oneself. Until we are able to basically live in those higher states, we need to put in the initial work to feel and understand what it means to be self-aware, that is, not controlled by our thoughts. After digesting a few more recordings and structuring my thoughts, I concluded that most "alternative" philosophies or worldviews stem from Eastern roots and seem to always touch on the teachings of Buddhism in one way or the other—i.e., everything is already inside us and (over)attachment to external factors will ultimately lead to suffering. I will not go into more detail as it would go beyond the scope of this book, but I think that anybody looking for more ease and comfort in their life, and who does not believe in other traditional religions, should take at least a look into those teachings, which can softly transform anyone's ability to approach life from a different perspective. However, one must be ready for and open to it.

While my weeks at home were very fruitful, I felt that I was ready to move on. I needed more time to continue my self-discovery process in peace. Given my dad was not feeling too good at that point, I wanted to stay near Germany to be able to come home anytime he needed me. I decided to go to Austria next—it was the perfect place to be: Spectacular mountains, beautiful small villages, old wooden houses, and a mix of sunny and snowy days. At the end of February, I took the train to Innsbruck, from where the journey began.

I continued journaling and implemented a routine for daily meditation. Everything I practiced was still intuitive; I never followed a step-by-step guide on "how to" but rather found my own way and style over time. For example, I would rarely sit in the typical lotus position that aims to help let the energy flow through the individual chakra centers, but rather lay comfortably down in bed, which provided me with the best bodily and sensory relaxation. Things were still a bit trial and error at that time, but thereby I established my best-working ways. In the end, meditation means nothing other than becoming present in the moment, mastering the mind to (temporarily) shut down all unconscious patterns, bypassing any system of thought. It means getting back into our natural state of pure awareness. Ergo, a very useful tool to reconnect with our source, recharge our batteries, and realign our inner chaos. With a bit of practice, it becomes pretty much a routine, like with anything else that we practice repeatedly.

One thing I noted was that I started to enjoy simply lying in the dark and being present, acting as the observer of my thoughts and feelings, acknowledging them without judging them, and letting them pass by. In the past, I would avoid such uncomforting situations at all costs as I wouldn't want to face all those painful thoughts/emotions/memories that naturally emerge in the state of stillness. However, in my opinion, this is one of the best ways to heal any mental wounds; I am avoiding the word "trauma" here as it might scare some people away. We often think of some extreme forms of violence or abuse in connection with it—nonetheless, we are all traumatized in one form or the other, and each one of us has unhealed wounds from the past. By simply observing (and not judging) these past events, which either pop up spontaneously in silent moments or can also be specifically targeted, one has the chance to feel through the emotions of the child or young adult from that time and thereby come to terms with what has happened. One will eventually be able to forgive either themself or the other person who (seemingly) caused the disturbing event, thereby detaching from it and becoming free. Note that trauma is a rather deep and complex topic in itself; I am not presuming to provide a professional guide on healing here but a simple approach that worked well for me and many others in non-severe cases. The interested reader may choose to read further on this topic.[2,3]

The bookshops in the cities and towns gave me a perfect place to read more on all topics related to spirituality without me having to buy and carry a load of books around in my backpack. I started to dive deeper into the differentiation of soul versus mind, de-identification of body and thoughts with the "true self", and intuitive living from the inside. These books were the perfect add-on for my previous high-level introductions from the digital recordings. Instead of just listening to summarizing views, I could pick books that would go into much more detail on specific aspects. At first, such specifics are rather hard to comprehend for someone (basically all of us?) who has been rationally trained and conditioned to perceive themselves as the "human body that thinks"; and this was also the case for me. What needs to happen is a fundamental reprogramming of our established belief system, which will usually not happen overnight. It won't immediately click by reading one book or listening to one recording. It is an exercise of repetition, digestion, and practical application—like any other new topic or activity that we learn—that we are individually responsible for. For me, it was the perfect setup. One by one, I went through the individual topics at a granular level. The clicks inside my brain became more frequent. With each one, I made new neuronal connections that prepared me for my first key event, which would follow a few weeks later.

I continued my travels through the beautiful scenery of the Zillertal: Mountain ranges crowned with snowy peaks to the left and right, a backdrop to the valley with quaint villages and farms. Everything nestled harmoniously in the embrace of the Alps. Almost postcard-like views in all directions. I took hour-long walks through the mountains and valleys, spending most of the time by myself. In my opinion, this is one of the most important factors one should consider when following the inner voice to liberation: Being able to spend time alone! Not only for a few hours but at least several days, or ideally multiple weeks. This whole process of inner healing, understanding, and growth is not an easy one and requires one's full attention to yield any meaningful results. How could you really feel and listen to the inside when you are constantly distracted and not silent or still? It is the most important foundation to build upon. The adaptation was not an easy one for me either, someone who had been constantly busy with work or weekend pleasures to avoid the discomfort of looking beyond the ego-self. However, step by step, I was able to let go and comfortably spend more time in silence.

The number of positive coincidences also increased at that time. You know, the feeling that everything works in your favor, specifically tailored toward you. It seems to just flow, no forcing; everything is naturally aligned. So it happened with the material I needed to find, read, and comprehend. In each small town I visited, I found public bookshelves that contained exactly those one or two additional books that fit my journey, that I had to read in order to round up my understanding of the topics of interest. In addition, I met exactly the right people at the right time, which gave me the opportunity to discuss, confirm, and apply my new knowledge in practice. Back then, I didn't particularly see or understand how all those things were related to each other, but I happily enjoyed that wonderful natural flow regardless. Today I know that none of those events were actually coincidences but rather synchronicities that I had (unconsciously) asked for.

Do you remember when I listened to *The Alchemist* in Greece a few months earlier? Now I had another book in my hands in which that main recurring theme popped up again, pointing me toward my next forthcoming lesson: The desert as a teacher—a place where one must face their own self to the depths. No distractions, no entertainment, no internet or mobile reception, and most importantly, no other people. Just total silence, sensory deprivation and monotony, and the helpers in need, the camels. In that moment, I knew exactly what I had to do; go to the desert next. The timing was perfect, as it becomes more dangerous and hotter in the months after March; scorpions are in hibernation under the dunes until March or April, and temperatures become basically unbearably thereafter. Still in Austria, I contacted a tour provider that helped me organize a team of two guides and two camels for a week-long marching trip through the desert in mid-April—I was really excited! Again, things seemed to just naturally flow, and the signs of guidance showed up left and right. I just had to follow them.

At my last stop in Austria, the key event finally happened: My first enlightenment. I was on a walk outside on a rather gray and rainy day, yet I felt good and somewhat light on my feet, like walking on clouds. I listened to another recording on the topic of soul versus mind, trying to digest how it all related to each other. For hours, I kept assembling the individual parts by repeating them to myself from all different angles and perspectives, and suddenly it clicked. The moment when I was no longer trying to understand the topic with my rationality but rather promptly felt it deep inside me as the truth; this was it. What had been dormant in me for years finally awakened. A moment of total clarity, a vivid state of bliss. No more questions or doubts. Just pure facts. I had accepted the new paradigm. Now everything made sense. I finally got it; I felt it! Of course I am not my body, I am not my thoughts, I am something everlasting, I am pure consciousness that persists, I am the soul—my life force.

I rushed back to my house, kept repeating and connecting the dots, and finally wrote it all down in my notebook. What a day, March 31, 2022; I had finally rediscovered my true essence. My first big aha moment, my first enlightenment. I spent the rest of the day in pure presence and happiness, doing nothing but humming and smiling. I felt content and humbled alike. I realized how little we truly know and how much there is still to discover.

What really helped me to reach the final click moment was the following example: You are moving your right hand up. You just do it, there is no thinking about it. But how does it exactly happen? A process occurs in the brain that sends out neurotransmitters into the respective body parts to activate the movement. That we can all scientifically agree on. However, who or what actually gives the brain the command to initiate that neurotransmitter release? Shouldn't there be something in control of all this? Consider a computer for comparison. It has all the necessary components to do the calculations and perform the requested activity—comparable to our human body when it lifts the right hand up. But there is still someone (in that case, a person) pushing the buttons on the computer keyboard, initiating the command. So, the question is, who or what could it be that initiates the command in us when we perform a certain activity? Surely none of us would like to think that our true self is the weirdly shaped, slimy mass of brain substance, right? Then there must be something else that represents the essence of what each one of us truly is at the core. That "something" is intangible and invisible—let us call it pure consciousness or the soul. The concept of the soul is a widely debated one which cannot be scientifically proven with the tools we have available at this point, and furthermore, it cannot be physically touched or grabbed. However, scientists around the world agree there is a higher center of awareness in the form of pure consciousness, even though its exact location or form is not yet determined—if it does indeed have one.

After this beautiful event, I thought that I got it. That I had cracked the "code of life". Little did I know that this was just the beginning. I had to go on and work through many different phases, from awakening to integration, over the months to follow. Only looking back did I realize how they differed and related to each other, but this is precisely how life works. If we were to characterize a "typical" enlightenment process, we could divide it into five or six key stages or phases. Note that their sequence, duration, and intensity will probably differ on a case-by-case basis; the phases below should be seen as a simplified framework.

Phase 1: Awakening

The critical starting point for the whole process to begin. For most people, there usually is one or a series of external trigger events that push our internal suffering and pain to a level that we can no longer bear. We deeply feel that we need to look for answers to life elsewhere, not in the physical or material world. It may be a breakup, the death of a family member, or a significant financial loss that forces us to break out of our old structures and beliefs. The ego is slowly dissolving, we start to disidentify with our thoughts and physical bodies, and finally rediscover our true self, the soul. The other, less common, way is a spontaneous awakening in the form of a sudden, abrupt "click"—without any specific external trigger events—and one realizes that they have lived their whole life in the illusion of the ego-self.

Phase 2: Bliss

The phase of bliss typically follows right after the actual awakening. We've just had this profound realization that we are much more than our thoughts or bodies and therefore feel extremely euphoric and conscious. It feels as if we finally understand what life is about. We feel oneness, as if we can mentally communicate with other people or animals. We are in a state of total connectedness, excited by the new "superpowers" we just discovered. A cocktail of joy, ecstasy, and bliss, with predominantly our heart and intuition in the driver's seat for probably the first time ever. Sometimes, we may even prematurely assume that the process is over, that we are done, already fully enlightened.

Phase 3: Dark Night

During this stage, the majority of the healing is taking place. All the negative and traumatic events from the past, starting from childhood to the most recent, will come up to be purged. Many of those things may have been hidden for years in our subconscious without us even realizing that we had a traumatic experience with or from it. It is a profound phase in the process as we let go and become "cleansed" of all pain, anxiety, or even depression that was buried inside us. Consequently, we experience a total shakeup of our emotions —we just came out of this beautiful bliss phase and are now faced with all these unpleasant aspects. We may feel as if we've lost control, as if we were about to die (our ego does). But, as with all things, this too shall pass. We have to sit through it. We have to face everything that needs healing. We have to acknowledge whatever comes up, devote our attention to it, feel what we have to feel, and then let go of it.

Phase 4: Emptiness

After we have released all these past traumatic experiences and hopefully let go of our ego-identification, we are somewhat in between the "old" self and the "new" self, which is yet to be formed. A stage of emptiness, comparable to a void. While before we felt so connected and at one with everything, we are now on our own. It is an interim period of nothingness. We try to find reasons for what is going on, may even blame others for it, or fall back into ego thinking patterns. This interim period is needed to rest and digest—whatever was released in the phases before was likely significant, and therefore our soul and body need time to adapt, time to form the new self.

Phase 5: Grounding and Integration

During this phase, we literally start coming back to ground again after we had previously grown above and beyond ourselves and the physical body. We become mature in the sense of leaving the need for bliss or ecstasy behind and realizing that we need to combine the two worlds of spirituality and human experience. We may ask ourselves how we should live our regular life now that we know that certain things, which we believed to be important, actually have little to no meaning. However, we start to realize that we are nevertheless on this planet to have selected experiences in our physical avatars. We accept and are ready to return to society, while in the previous phases, we were more likely to withdraw. We are now able to integrate what we have learned into our daily lives.

Phase 6: Life Mission

I would consider this phase as the "cherry on top" and hence it's somewhat optional. Not everyone is able or willing to define a completely new life mission or purpose for themselves going forward. This stage would impact and dictate the rest of our lives if we chose to follow it wholeheartedly. After we have significantly transformed during phases 1–5, and most likely rediscovered our self-love and love for others, we may choose to realign our profession, relationships, and general life structure with those new values and principles. A less drastic alternative would be to make selected changes in our lives where needed while taking them one step at a time.

For me personally, the whole process took a bit more than a year. If you follow along with the story throughout the book, you will be able to recognize the individual phases and their characteristics along the way. Phase 1 was the key day at my last stop in Austria, described earlier in the chapter. While the preparation or buildup of events had already taken place the year before (financial losses, pleasure traps, etc.), the actual awakening happened just then. Phase 2 was basically from there on until the end of my Morocco trip. The time when I felt so much bliss, guidance, and connectedness with everything. Phase 3 started simultaneously during my Morocco trip, with the turbulent night in the Atlas Mountains being one prominent example of purge. It lasted throughout Portugal and Norway until the death of my dad. Phase 4 was mostly my time in Asia, where I was a bit lost and in between the worlds. Whereas I had been filled with insights and intuition during the months before, I had by then seemingly lost the connection to my inner self and thus distracted myself with pleasure. Phase 5 really started during my Central and South America trip, where I also met S. I knew my journey was coming to an end, and I felt ready to combine spiritual insights with daily life, preparing for my return to society. Phase 6 began in Switzerland, where I finally found my new guiding principle in life, my North Star, that I had previously lost. I decided to write this book, with which I hope to set the foundation for exactly that.

As mentioned before, the sequence and duration of these phases are highly individualistic and shouldn't be seen as a one size fits all. However, through many conversations and reports or testimonials, I have found that this framework is somewhat general enough to fit most cases. To conclude, the whole enlightenment process is fairly turbulent and life-altering, but that should not come as a surprise. After all, we are changing significantly from the inside, realizing that our ego-self is nothing but a predominantly society-driven construct. And that needs time to be digested, accepted, and integrated.

While we are born as "pure" creatures without an ego-identity, undisturbed by thought patterns and capable of living in the moment, we unfortunately unlearn this way of life over the years, only to relearn it a few decades later. Let us together consider the typical way this unfolds from birth to death as an example. When we watch a baby or young kid up to the age of five or six play, we can usually observe how much joy and fulfillment they have in doing whatever they do. They don't think about the consequences, they don't care about what others think; all they want is to fully enjoy what they are doing. They are totally present, conscious in the moment. Then, at the latest when it is time to go to school, this beautiful phenomenon will change. We tell them to behave in a certain way, do certain things, and say specific words. We don't accept them not obeying our rules. We force a narrowness on them that basically teaches them: If you don't behave like mommy and daddy tell you to, we won't love you. Of course, no parents would ever verbalize those exact words, but the message gets delivered by their actions, nonetheless. The kid comes home with bad grades, doesn't want to eat the vegetable soup, or destroys the new trousers while playing outside, and suddenly, mommy and daddy behave differently. Suddenly there is less love, less attention, and less empathy than there was before. These are just a few common examples, but the list is never-ending. I am sure each one of us, being a parent or not, will thoroughly remember and feel many of those situations from our own childhood.

So, the years pass by, and the child develops what they need for their own protection: Ego identity. The identity that helps them think and evaluate rationally what they should or should not do in order to be loved, to be accepted. They develop patterns and habits that are aligned with those of mom and dad to avoid conflict and discomfort or, put differently, to seek comfort. A need for control emerges, controlling themself, others, and situations around them, to ensure as much acceptance and pain avoidance as possible. The ego-self is born. From here on, our lives are basically in the hands of our ego, some more and some less, but they all are. For some, these patterns even last until adulthood and throughout their whole professional careers. They are still the hardworking, perfectionist, and often narcissistic individuals who (subconsciously) follow the early-adopted thinking mechanisms of "I have to be the best, then I will be accepted and regarded well," "I need to be perfect, otherwise I will not be loved," or "I need to control this situation, otherwise I may face pain and neglect." It may sound a bit harsh to bluntly put it like that, but it ultimately is what oftentimes happens. I realized the same patterns in myself when I finally stopped and spent a (long) moment in silence.

However, sooner or later, each one of us will come to a point where we ask ourselves if there is no more to life than just the way we are typically living it—tailored to our ego-identity. For many people, that point comes around their forties or fifties, when their career doesn't progress as much anymore, and when the kids are out of the house. A longing for more begins. We want to go back to the old times when we could simply enjoy the moment, not constantly bombarded by thoughts and fears about everyone and everything in our lives. We simply want to be at peace again. We want to feel calm and whole. We want the rush to stop. And then the journey to the inside commences. Step by step, we realize that we have unlearned this beautiful, trusting way of living that we used to have as kids. We realize how strict, narrow, and repetitive our belief systems have become. How we have lived the last years or decades in illusion. Each one of us must find our own way to reach the decision point: I want to rediscover my true essence and relearn the detached way of life beyond the ego-mind. And from there on, it depends on us individually. At some point before death, we have to face the situation. There is no way around it. In the end, we are all the same.

Summing it up, we typically go through three periods in life. First, we are allowed to grow up "in the moment" with a less strict focus on manners and behaviors, typically in the first few years. Next, mostly around the time school starts, the ego-self will get into the driver's seat and likely remain there for decades. It dictates the way we act, think, and feel, all in order to maximize our comfort. Last, we want to unlearn those ego-tailored patterns and relearn how to live in trust and presence instead, rediscovering our true essence and preparing our "way back" to death. It is not always an easy journey, but ultimately one we all have to make. I speak from my own experience; I went through all three stages myself—just a bit earlier than the average.

One last anecdote I would like to mention is that I continuously saw ravens at every place I went to in Austria. They were flying over me on my walks, they were sitting on the transmission poles close to the benches I paused on, they were landing next to me while I was randomly outside, and they were gathering on house antennas in front of the balconies of my rooms. I will not aim to provide an interpretation of what exactly this could have meant, or if it had a meaning at all, but at that time it gave me a feeling of guidance and trust; it confirmed that I was on the right track. A phenomenon I have, to that extent, encountered in only one other country during my two years of travel: Switzerland.

The next day, I took the train home and spent two weeks with my family and my dad. His condition was volatile in the sense that he had some good days and some bad days, but overall, he was still okay and managed the situation with a bit of help. We had a few nice breakfasts (one of our traditions) and coffees and cakes together; he agreed that I should take the trip to the desert and most definitely needed to send him the pictures and impressions afterward. I packed my things, bought a light wind jacket, sunscreen, and a headlamp, and departed for Morocco a few days later.

Max Tower

I stayed three days in the bustling Old Town of Marrakesh, which has its own charming vibe but is a rather busy and noisy place full of souvenir merchants and tourists. A maze of narrow alleys that make you trot around for hours in the souks (local markets) with only little chance to find a way out. While I was a bit overwhelmed at first, I began to love its lively atmosphere in the following days. Each day I would walk through the markets, drink tea at my regular café, and chat with the owner or some of the merchants about whatever came to mind. Maybe I should have opened a souvenir stand in the souks myself—my bargaining skills weren't so bad after all. Then my trip to the Sahara began, a twelve-hour bus ride through the Atlas Mountains. It was a rather old bus with no air conditioning and little ventilation, though at least the seat next to me was free, and I had enough space to make myself comfortable. The whole bus was fully booked besides the seat next to me and one other. At the interim stops, some people got out, and some new people got in—one of them a guy from Denmark. All the other passengers were just local people on the way to their villages, and the only other foreigner booked the seat right next to me. In the beginning, I was not really amused, as I wanted to have the most real and local experiences possible, but it turned out to be the perfect time and place to meet him. We started talking about our journeys, and he unveiled to be a rather interesting character: He described himself as a forty-year-old mind in the body of a twenty-five-year-old guy, and after talking with him for several hours, I tended to agree.

Two Years

His worldview and way of living were pretty untypical for someone his age. For example, he drank no alcohol, enjoyed no entertainment, watched no porn, valued his privacy, and traveled with only a tiny rucksack that contained two pairs of underwear, socks, T-shirts, and pullovers. Besides that, only a small blanket, a compass, and a refillable drinking bottle. He traveled old-school style and preferred to use the compass over digital maps on the phone, sometimes slept outside in parks under trees, and generally made sure to use as little technology as possible. While talking to him, it became clear that he'd had certain experiences that made him form this advanced character; I offered to just listen and added a few anecdotes of my journey to balance the conversation with a different perspective on life. This was probably exactly what both of us needed at that time, to take on new views and mindsets for our travels ahead. I learned about another "extreme" form of travel and that there is nothing to be afraid of, while he understood the need to turn inward to find the root of his adopted patterns. After five more hours, we finally reached the small gateway town of Mhamid, right at the beginning of the desert. One of the guides picked me up, took me to the house where I slept that night, and the next morning our trip started.

The two camels were packed, the two guides ready, and I put on my turban for sun and sand protection. An exciting week of purity and nothingness lay right ahead of us. One of the guides spoke a little English so we could communicate when needed, but we mostly understood each other without much talking anyway. Also, what is there really to talk about in the desert on eight-hour-long daily walks? It was time to look deeper inside, just me versus myself. The days were structured as follows: Walk four hours in the morning, find a place to rest during the afternoon sun, unpack the camels, and prepare lunch. Then pack the camels and continue to walk for another four hours, find a place to put up the tents for the night, unpack the camels again, and prepare dinner. A procedure of total simplicity, a beauty in the monotony of each day. It was Ramadan at that time, and the two guides stuck strictly to the no drinking and no eating before sunset stricture for the first two days, but eventually had to give in a little as the daily walking in the hot desert sun became somewhat torturous without at least drinking some water.

On our second day, the wind started to set in more strongly. As you can imagine, in the beginning, it annoyed me quite a bit, given we as Westerners are used to always keeping ourselves tidy and clean in the comfortable and protective environment of the "civilized world". I tried to keep my eyes and mouth clean as well as possible, emptied my shoes of sand every half-hour or so, and was indecisive between keeping my wind jacket with a hood on but sweat a ton or sticking with the turban that would regularly loosen but be at least more comfortable temperature wise. Walk. Stop. Clean eyes and mouth. Take a sip of water. Continue walking. Push through. Stop. Empty shoes. Tighten turban. Continue walking. Keep fighting. Stop. Take turban off. Put wind jacket on. More walking. The first few hours of this procedure were almost fun and felt like an adventure or challenge, but after two days of constant wind and sand bombardment, my mood naturally took a hit; I felt anger and despair coming up inside me. Why does

Two Years

the sandstorm need to come up exactly now? Will this last the entire week? Why can't things go smoothly for once? Why is there always something going wrong? I didn't like or appreciate the circumstance I was in. I wanted to change it. Wanted to get control of the situation. However, I reminded myself that there was literally nothing I could do about it. What benefit would it bring me to be angry at the powers of nature, the desert, or the circumstance itself? Right, there was exactly zero benefit—there was no escaping this situation, anyway. What I needed to do was simply take on "what is" without an illusory judgment of good or bad, positive or negative, and just remain present as the observer of the events instead of being identified with them. At this turning point, I learned the next important lesson on my travels: Acceptance.

We need to accept what we cannot change and which does not cross the boundaries of morality, of course. While conflict (of ideas and beliefs) is how we can move forward as a society in general, acceptance of immutable or definitive circumstances in life are equally important. We need to accept that we are imperfect, accept that we lost a loved one, accept that our partner broke up with us, accept that our children will go their own ways, and accept our financial decisions. Only by letting go of attachments to certain (past) situations, (present) moments, or (future) expectations can we become truly free and accept whatever we encounter in life. We stop seeking wholeness or happiness from the external world—circumstances, people, etc.—and find it within ourselves instead. This is precisely what I had to do during those days of sandstorm. Of course, the sand was everywhere—in the nose, in the mouth, in the eyes, in the hair, in the shoes, in the socks, and in the underwear. But there was absolutely no way to win this fight with the desert. The only way was to accept it and adapt to it. I felt relieved once I changed my attitude toward the circumstances I faced; I didn't mind any longer spitting out sand, blowing it out of my nose, or fishing it out of any other parts of my body. I even peacefully napped while the sand blew right into my face. I resigned myself to the superiority of nature, gave up control, and became more and more fascinated by the sincerity of the Sahara—its power to mirror one's own shortcomings to work on. After the third day, the wind eventually passed, and we continued our march in peace and silence without the constant whistling noise of it.

The total silence in the desert was what I learned to love the most. Besides the occasional wind and the footsteps from our small group, there was literally no noise at all. Nothing. Not even the slightest sound. Zero distractions. Something that most of us are not used to anymore thanks to constant external noises such as traffic, television, music, and talking, or even internal noise coming from (unconscious) mind chatter. Once all these things are stripped away, there is nothing but a beautiful, lasting silence that provides an ideal opportunity to become fully present in the moment. The internal mind chatter may be there initially but will slowly pass to make space for the big nothingness ahead. What a peaceful environment to be in.

Over the days, I became very close with the camels. These animals are such fascinating creatures, so calm, so modest, so patient. They carry all the baggage, water, and food but don't even need any water themselves. During the whole time, they did not drink even once; only after we returned to Mhamid did they refill their internal water systems. Also, camels are ruminants, which means they "recycle" the food they eat multiple times by throwing it up and chewing it down again. In the beginning, this phenomenon may seem a little disgusting or strange, but one learns to see the beauty in it as it makes the camels the perfect helpers for a long trip through the desert. During the nights, I would occasionally wake up, and the only thing I heard was the camels chewing their food, which gave me a feeling of comfort and safety. The slow, rhythmic sound of the chewing process was almost hypnotic and sent me back to sleep immediately. In the mornings, I would usually wake up first and walk around to explore the area we'd camped in for the night. My two hairy friends were also awake already at that time, and I would go to greet and pet them before my explorations, thereby tightening our bond. It is an indescribable feeling to just sit on a dune, watch the sunrise, and be automatically in a meditative state without even purposely attempting to do so. Deathlike stillness except the soft buzzing ground noise of our own ears, miles away from all civilization, with total connectedness to the inner self. Such pure, non-replicable moments. After the two guides woke up (they usually stayed awake longer due to Ramadan), we prepared for the day, packed the camels, and continued on our way.

On a side note, I would like to mention how diverse in scenery the Sahara actually is. The different types of vegetative landscapes stretch over several miles and are way more than the big dunes that we typically think of. For example, we crossed totally flat Death-Valley-like areas where the ground was hard and broken into large plates of dry sand, and parts that looked like steppes with occasional bushes and small trees growing out of the hilly land, and some territories with the pure, fine sand dunes reaching as far as the eye can see. An immense amount of diversity covered by a deceiving shell of uniformity. Something quite transferable to other situations in life.

Our nightly rituals were my favorite moments of the trip. We would sit on the rugs in the sand, prepare our daily campfire to cook dinner and boil tea, and appreciate the breathtaking star-filled sky that the Sahara has to offer. The energy bond between the three of us, the camels, and the desert itself was so strong that there was not even the slightest (irrational) fear of scorpions, snakes, or other animals. We sat in the dark, only the thin rugs between our bodies and the sand, and we walked around barefoot, trusting that everything was all right. For them, it was routine; for me, it was a beautiful symbiosis of everything around me. There was no thinking, there was no worrying, there was no judging. There was simply this one beautiful moment. One after the other. Each with its own perfection. A sequence of magnificent snapshots that formed our own movie. After we ate and drank our tea, we would lie down and look up at the sky, silent, together, but each one for himself. Never in my life have I experienced clearer, more glowing, or more stunning skies filled with stars than during those nights. The stars appeared so close as to almost be able to grab them, so shiny that it never got totally dark, and so orderly that it was easy to spot any formations on the first attempt. These moments I will certainly never forget—everything just became one. Thank you, Sahara!

On the last day we headed back to Mhamid and met a group of other people who had booked a day tour in a jeep. We shared lunch together and mainly talked about my experiences of the last week, what brought me on this trip, and what I took away from it for the future. I felt good and sad at the same time to see other people again: Good to talk with someone in full sentences again, good to feel the satisfaction of "I made it, no more walking, wind, and sand," and good to sense the first shower in days just hours away. Sad to be coming back to civilization with all its noise, superficiality, and chaos again, sad to say goodbye to my amazing new friends (the two guides and camels), and sad to leave my teacher, the desert with all its purity, behind. That day I promised myself that I would definitely come back in the future. Note that I would highly recommend a multi-day solo desert trip for anyone with a real intention of working on themself and no chance of backing out; in my opinion, there are not many comparable alternatives that offer this unique experience as well as the therapeutic effect in equal parts. One has to face their own thoughts and emotions to the depths; there is literally no way to escape—the only way out is to deal with it. By walking, by crying, by screaming, by allowing, and by healing. There is no one and nothing that would judge, interfere, or prevent the healing process. There is only you and the desert.

We walked for a few more hours and finally reached Mhamid, where the camels got their chance to drink, and I was able to thoroughly clean my body under a steady stream of water. As the town was so rural and mystic at the same time, I decided to stay another two days to peacefully digest my experiences in the right environment. I journaled a lot, ate fantastic traditional food that tempted my taste buds each time anew (I especially liked all variations of tagine and couscous), and sent my family the promised pictures. Then I had to think about my next destination and decided that I should stay in rural Morocco for a bit longer—somehow, I totally connected with the people here and always felt like one of them rather than just a tourist visiting them. Hence, I booked a room in a family house in the town of Aslim for the next four days.

The tiny village consisted of a few traditional houses made of mud. Half of them were ruins and abandoned, while the other half were filled with friendly, caring families that lived their lives the traditional way. My host family was used to having international guests, and the father spoke quite good English. I basically became a part of their family for these few days, which was such a wonderful experience. Each night we shared a delicious Moroccan dinner together with three generations, up to ten people, in one room. Afterward, we usually went outside to play with the kids of the village. Occasionally, I would sit with the father of the family, talking about everything from music to global politics while enjoying a tasty digestive tea and some fine local hash. With the rest of the family, I communicated the old-school way with hands and feet. For example, with the grandma of the house, who made sure I never left without eating at least two portions. The kids didn't need much talking anyway; we just ran, jumped around, and played games together.

Those times with kids, playing soccer or frisbee in the dusty, rocky center of the town, were among my favorite moments there. It didn't matter that the soccer ball was years old and already falling apart, it didn't matter that the frisbee disk was just an old bucket lid, and it certainly didn't matter that I was the only foreign person in the group of Moroccan boys and girls. Such a beautiful dynamic each day—no talking was needed at all. We simply understood each other by playing fun games. Some of the village kids also had to work in the fields, lead loaded donkeys up the hills, or pursue work in and around the houses. Life was very basic around here, but the level of joy I experienced from these young boys and girls was largely incomparable to the average Western kid around their age. There was more appreciation for the moment, more gratitude for the little materialistic things they had, and more acceptance of the circumstances they lived in. There was a general sense of "we" mentality rather than "me versus them" mentality in this town, a collective of people working together as a group rather than individuals competing against each other. With so little available, we felt so much joy! A contrast I hadn't experienced to this degree for a long time, if ever. I was very thankful for my time in Aslim as these kids taught me the next key lesson: Gratitude.

I needed to be happy with what I had. Yes, there is always something new or more exciting to go after, but does it really benefit us? I circled back to all the financial losses I had taken during the last year and realized that what I dreamed of buying with it was simply time—time to do whatever I want, when I want, where I want, and with whom I want. Ironically, this was exactly what I had achieved thanks to all the events of the last year, which led me to this point. A feeling of satisfaction came over me as I could finally see and connect the events of the past year from a different perspective. I was grateful for everything that happened, grateful for all the things that I learned, grateful for the wonderful people I met, and grateful for this moment.

On the last day, I bought a new soccer ball for the village so that the kids could keep playing for years to come and hopefully retain the joy I had met them with. As we played one last round with this ball, even the girls above a certain age joined in and kicked around with us; this was not a very common phenomenon, given the rather strict religious and cultural values in the rural areas of the country. Therefore, I was even happier to also see them laugh, smile, and enjoy the moment together with the rest of us. My time to leave had come, and the goodbye was certainly an emotional one. The host family and kids gave me warm hugs, and the grandma added several cheek kisses on top—everyone had gathered to wave after me for my departure.

For the next three days, I stopped at a small campsite where I was the only guest and once again had the chance to become a part of the family, sharing dinner each night and playing with their two kids. As per the father, the campsite used to be always busy in the past, and many tourists would come with their campervans to stay for a couple of days on their way through Morocco. He showed me old pictures of the site packed with vans, jeeps, and regular cars, with not a single bit of free space available. Post Covid, the tourism recovery was somewhat slow—something that I had also noticed along my way. However, he didn't seem too worried about it; he trusted it would get better soon. After this conversation, I kept thinking about the idea of living in a van or a bit, something that had never been super appealing to me in the past, but my mindset seemed to have changed over the last months. I was more open to trying new things of all sorts, and the thought of being totally flexible and mobile at the same time suddenly became attractive. I thought about my sister's old van that she had bought a few months before and with which she toured through Europe for a while. But I didn't want to take on the burden of that untrustworthy, dodgy vehicle that regularly broke down somewhere on the road. I concluded that it would be better to simply rent a van for a few weeks to maximize flexibility and minimize responsibility. I updated J on the van idea, she liked it, and we agreed that we should tour in a van through Portugal in June. We spent the next day on the phone comparing providers, prices, and services and swiftly agreed on the best option. Amazing—the next adventure was already planned, and an eventful summer lay ahead.

My last stop on the way back to Marrakesh was high up in the Atlas Mountains, the awe-inspiring mountain range stretching across several countries in North Africa. Home to many Berber families, these mountains separate the Sahara from the Mediterranean and Atlantic coast of the continent. The perfect playground for various outdoor activities, especially trekking or hiking. Instead of camels, donkeys are the helpers in need on those steep and rocky hills. I booked a room in a riad for another three days and was the only guest besides a local couple on their honeymoon. I met the owner of the house, checked in, and went outside to do my usual exploration walks of the area. I strolled through the small town, greeted the friendly people, climbed up the rocks, and finally reached the mountaintop. Nice, calming scenery with fresh, unpolluted air all around, and then I spotted it—a homemade soccer field right on top of the mountain. Homemade in the sense of having neither walls at the sides nor a net in the goal. The ball would simply blow through the goal or out of the field to left or right and all the way down the hill. Fascinating. A few boys from the town saw me standing on the field and ran right up to me with a ball to play. I lost count after the fifth time these guys practically went flying down the rocky hills to catch the ball every time it missed the goal or blasted right through it. No fear, total precision, and that in sandals! In that moment, I remembered how fearless I had been as a young boy. Jumping stairs, handrails, and half pipes on my skateboard without even thinking about any potential consequences; how many times I broke my bones or had to get stitches. While increased caution and rationality are normal characteristics of growing up, maybe we could all use a little detox from fear and overthinking on occasion—after all, we trusted our body with all its abilities our whole life, right? Absent any specific physical or mental reasons, nothing should have changed. I reminded myself to keep it present for my remaining journey. A few matches later, I thanked the boys and went back to take a hot shower, have dinner, and prepare for a relaxed evening. However, this first night in the mountain riad turned out to be anything but relaxing or regular—it literally shook me up from the inside. What was about to happen played a key role in my further development to finally dissolve my old ego-identity, to cleanse and connect my inner energy centers, and to reaffirm my envisaged way of life going forward.

Everything was quite normal at first—I had a beer on the roof, enjoyed the view and fresh air of the mountains, and patiently waited for dinner time while chatting with the honeymoon couple about Morocco and its people. The food was prepared by the "watcher" of the house; it was a tasty traditional soup and a huge tagine. We ate, drank tea, and afterward, I went to my room to digest. I remembered that I had some hash left that the dad of the Aslim family gave me for the rest of my trip. I rolled a tiny one, smoked it in a few puffs, and lay down in bed with soft background music. From here on, things started to get very interesting, to say the least.

First, I closed my eyes as usual and followed the depths of the harmonic and calming rhythm, gliding into deep relaxation. Then, out of nowhere, a sticky nervousness came up inside me, and my mind started racing intensely. A big load of repetitive, negative thoughts burst right over me, and I had absolutely no idea where it came from after such a wonderful day. The negative thoughts along the lines of "What are you even doing here? None of this makes sense!" "What about your future? You don't even have any plans!" or "You think last year was a good decision? You are trying to kid yourself!" became more intense with every passing minute. They had such a negative connotation to them that I got deeper and deeper down the spiral and eventually could no longer regain control of my mind—it controlled me. While this may sound like a form of anxiety attack at first, I knew that it was something much more intense, something that I had never experienced before. My heart was racing so fast and beating so strongly that I really thought I might have a heart attack at any moment—never before had I felt such an intense and unrhythmic pounding in my chest. So unpleasant and "hostile" that I would have given anything to make it stop.

The thoughts became narrower and more confusing; nothing made sense anymore. I couldn't stop it, and with each attempt, the intensity seemed to escalate even further. At this point, I knew that I had lost control—I was helpless, at the mercy of whatever was in charge. Until I hit the peak and, for a few minutes, forgot who I was. I could obviously see me, the person, lying on the bed, trying to make sense of the situation, but I had no sense of who that person was. Imagine the everyday feeling of you being "you" (the parent, doctor, athlete, etc., of a certain age and persona) being completely gone, and all that is left is consciousness in a body that you don't know, that you cannot sort into a known template any longer. That is exactly what happened to me in this situation: My ego-identity completely dissolved. I was scared. I was nervous. And I panicked.

Next, I tried to smoke a cigarette on the balcony to calm myself down; I wrapped the blanket around myself and took one step in front of the door. The night temperature was so cold that I didn't even light the cigarette and immediately went back inside. I went to the bathroom to wash my face and returned to bed, covered under the blanket. Now my body began to shake uncontrollably. Initially, I thought this must have come from the cold outside, but it was too intense and uncontrollable for too long. For several minutes my legs shook as if they were under electric shocks, which then gradually made their way up to my main body. I tried to stop it. No success. I tried to control it. No chance either. I even tried to enhance it, but my body would not "listen" to my commands. There was literally nothing I could do. An unstoppable vibration that I could not master—I had to fully surrender, and all I eventually did was watch. Watch the events as observer, as the consciousness, in the body that was out of my control. Nevertheless, the irrational fears and questions continued: "What is going on? Am I going crazy? Did the watcher put drugs in the food? Was it the hash? Why does this have to happen here in the mountains? Will I die? And who am I?" Confusion. Lethargy. Helplessness. I couldn't make any sense of this at all. Here I was, a person not knowing who he is, looking at his body severely shaking, not being able to identify the cause. For sure a great situation to be in.

Then I decided to slowly read a few articles on my phone in an attempt to get my sense of reality back. Everything was too much at first, the light, the colors, the letters. Nevertheless, I kept pushing myself until I was capable of actually reading a few lines. And it seemed to work; after a few minutes I calmed down and could identify "me" again. What a relief! Gradually I got my identity back—I remembered who I was, what my name was, how old I was, and where I lived. That was all I wanted, and I got it. Slowly my heart rate went down, my thoughts stopped racing, and I reminded myself that whatever was happening here tonight, I would get through this by myself and not go to the hospital.

By now the body vibrations were mostly over, and I felt slightly more comfortable in my situation. What followed next was a different, less intense bodily sensation; it was softer, warmer, and more orderly. There was this sensation of a "ball of energy" making its way through my body, pausing for several minutes at each station before moving on to the next. It started in the area below my stomach, where this energy cluster stayed for around twenty minutes; all remaining parts of the body became meaningless or nonexistent during that time, my full attention on this area only. The pulsations were strong but also comforting because now there was no more uncontrollable shaking or fear, just pure awareness of this "thing" moving through me.

Afterward, it came up to my chest, where it also stayed for several minutes. The sensation was still the same as before—a bundle of energy residing wherever it chose to stop. It appeared that the threat was over, and a feeling of familiarity had replaced it. I could finally relax, close my eyes, and begin to enjoy what was happening: A pleasant pulsation of energy located in my chest, rhythmically aligned with the beating of my heart. A beautiful coherence. It felt good to be mostly in control of my body again and not on the brink of a heart attack anymore. Even though I was not sure of what exactly was crawling up inside me, I felt that I could trust it and surrendered to the situation.

The final notable destination was my head—at the sides, on the forehead, and on top of it. The energy bundle created a tingling sensation all around the head, almost friendly and most definitely harmless. I remained calm and simply enjoyed the slow, harmonic oscillations. At this point, there were no more thoughts at all, only focused awareness on the individual parts of my head, one after the other, in an orderly manner. The intensity gradually declined, and after another fifteen minutes, it was almost gone. After the sensations eventually passed, my body was totally still. I felt that this was it, no more would come. A feeling of trust that I could fully let go. It felt good. I liked it. Almost like reborn. I turned to the side, covered myself in the blanket, and patiently waited to fall asleep. I was completely exhausted, with no more physical or mental capacity to digest anything further. In total, the whole procedure lasted around three hours. What a crazy night!

I woke up surprisingly well-rested the next morning and was happy to feel like myself again. I took a shower, went downstairs for breakfast, and asked the watcher of the house if he had put something in my food or tea. He looked at me, surprised, and denied it. Then what happened to me last night? Was it because of the tiny amount of hash? That couldn't be it. I had smoked it before without any issues. Was it really just the cold that made me shake so uncontrollably? That couldn't be it either. I never felt such an intensity before. Or was it an anxiety attack after all? No, it was something else. I couldn't solve the mystery at that moment, but that didn't really matter. What mattered was that it was over and that I felt like myself again. Yet something had changed—there was still a slight feeling of fear and uncertainty inside me, but I decided to brush it off and take a walk to the mountaintop. On the way up, I reconstructed the events of the last night and somehow felt "two sides" polarizing inside me: The first, the fearful, rational side, said, "You should listen to the racing thoughts from last night as they show you the way back to the normal life where you belong." The second, the trusting and intuitive side, said, "Continue the path you are on—what happened last night was a slip back to the old ego-self that tried to regain control over you." I was undecided; maybe I should stop the travel now and acknowledge that it was time to return to a regular life, but on the other hand, I made such big steps in my personal growth over the last year and probably shouldn't let this one event push me off my path.

I sat down on a wall close to the top, overlooking the valley, and stared into the sky. I didn't purposely attempt to get into a deeper meditative state. I just wanted to feel inside what the "real" me was—the first or the second side. After a while in stillness, I regained my confidence and knew: It was number two! I didn't need to think about it rationally, I didn't need to make a pro and con list, and I didn't need to consult anybody else. I simply knew it intuitively. That was it. The way of life I wanted to live. Happy about that realization, I sat on the wall for another few minutes and promised myself that I would no longer let my ego-mind interfere with my new approach to life. That I would use it as a tool going forward (when I want and decide to) instead of it using me. I concluded that last night happened for a reason; it was a test, a manifestation, that I had to experience to continue on my path as the new me. Whatever it was that made its way through my body helped me to let go of my ego attachment. In that moment, I remembered a quote from Eckhart Tolle that I found very fitting for this occasion: "The secret of life is to die before you die." This does not mean that from this point onward my ego was completely dead, but I understood what it means to surrender and to let go. Letting go of the attachment to an artificial and illusory identity created by society.

On my way back down, I called J to tell her about what had occurred the night before. It felt good to share those events and emotions with someone, and it reassured me that I did not go crazy; it had indeed happened. Back in the riad, I started sweating and coughing and fell sick for the next two days. I didn't care much at that point because all I wanted was to rest and relax. I mostly stayed in my room and only took short walks to buy water and food. In the morning on the last day, I felt almost back to normal and ready to return to Marrakesh. The watcher called me a taxi, and off I went—what an intense three days it had been.

Back in Marrakesh, I stayed at the same cozy and calm riad in Medina as I did before. I told the owners—who had almost become friends by that time—about all that had happened; we laughed a lot together over a tasty cup of tea. I still wondered if maybe the hash I had smoked that night in the mountains had something to do with the events. I needed to make sure and decided that I should carefully smoke the leftovers to confirm. I went to my room, smoked it, and afterward spent hours meditating. I felt total trust in myself and my promise to continue as the new version of myself. During these hours, for the first time, I felt a glimpse of real divinity. A sincere form of wholeness, connectedness, and love for everyone. It was such an intense and beautiful sensation that tears of joy were rolling down my cheeks. I felt deep compassion for all individuals and realized that everyone is acting from their own level of consciousness, and some simply don't know better (yet). There was no point judging, confronting, or countering other ego-identities with my own ego; what I needed to do instead was open myself from a perspective of love. To be the best version of myself. To be the new me. This heartwarming experience was a wonderful add-on to my actual goal to confirm that the hash had nothing to do with the other night. I was happy and enjoyed my last day at the riad before flying home at the beginning of May.

Summing it up, Morocco really had a significant impact on my personal development during my travels—basically everything that happened in that country was insightful, meaningful, and transformative. I am really grateful that I followed my intuition to the Sahara and took it step by step from there without any fixed plans. It was such an honest and emotional trip that contributed considerably to my new perspective on and way of life. Over the months to follow, I spent hours reading reports and testimonials of experiences similar to mine from that night in the Atlas Mountains. I concluded that it was a form of Kundalini awakening[4,5]—the energy that rests dormant at the base of the spine. In my interpretation, the heavy shaking was some form of trauma release that had been stored in my body, potentially for years. It served as a preparation for the Kundalini to awaken and to subsequently travel up my spine, thereby cleansing and activating all energy centers, or chakras, along the way. My ego-identity (temporarily) died that night, preparing the way for the new me to set in.

Two Years

In Germany, I spent a wonderful week with family, handed everyone the presents I brought from all over Morocco, and enjoyed some lovely breakfasts, walks, and mini-golf games with my dad. His condition was overall unchanged, with some good and some bad days. Though by now the summer had arrived, and he could at least spend more time outside, in the garden, watching the birds. I got the feeling that he'd started to slowly accept that at some point things would take their turn, but the fighter in him kept going to make the best out of this, probably last, summer. When I look back, I think he purposely fought toward his seventy-fourth birthday in July, which he wanted to celebrate for one last time. It was not an easy position to be in for him—someone who had always been in top condition his whole life, who had served as a role model at the federal police for decades, who had successfully competed in all varieties of running sports in top ranks, and who almost never needed to see a doctor—to let go of that identity and life he had breathed in and out since he was a teenager. However, we also couldn't just dump these rather "heavy" spiritual topics on him in his sick condition, and he wasn't internally ready to seek this path; we tried with a few hints here and there, but ultimately, he found his own way to deal with everything, which was perfectly fine. I had learned not to force my views or opinions on others but to be available for conversations when asked instead. One thing I am very thankful for is the fact that we could spend so much time together so regularly. If I had still been in NYC at that point, I would have had significantly less flexibility to fly home frequently and spend time with him, if at all. Luckily, I was free instead, and we met in between each of my trips. In a certain sense, it was a harmonic constitution of circumstances. A blessing in disguise.

In mid-May, J and I met in Lisbon to pick up our temporary home, the van, for the next four weeks. The instructions were clear and the van was easy to drive. After a bit of back and forth to find our working rhythm, in the sense of J checking and reading the map and directing me where to drive, we were genuinely excited for the weeks ahead. A feeling of being totally free in nature, no moving between apartments, no trains or taxis, just one consistent roof yet fully flexible in location. We made our way out of the busy city center, stocked up at the next supermarket, and started our trip north up the coast: Golden sandy beaches stretching along the azure Atlantic Ocean, soothing sound of waves hitting the shore, and a salty sea breeze carrying hints of marine freshness. The windows open. Music on. Wind in our hair. Freedom!

We usually drove for a maximum of three hours per day, then looked for our perfect spot to camp, bought groceries, explored the area, prepared dinner, and relaxed. A totally simple way of life—the only thing to do was buy groceries on the way, cook, and eat. As you can imagine, the most beautiful moments were the mornings and the sunsets at night. In the mornings, we simply opened the van's back door and immediately heard the ocean waves and birds (depending on location) that would peacefully wake us up and let us be in this perfect moment for a bit longer. We watched the sun rise, leading its first energizing waves of light to our faces. Nothing on the to-do list, just fully appreciating the morning in its own glory. After a while, we would get up, have breakfast, and discuss the plan

Two Years

for the day—stay one more night or find a new location. At night, the procedures were similar, but with a higher focus on dinner preparation and watching the sunsets, alone or in groups with other travelers. In the past, I never took regular time to cook my own food, mainly due to efficiency. Here it was different. We really appreciated the simple acts of cutting and preparing the veggies, meat or fish, and other ingredients. It was another exercise to be fully present, enjoying what we were doing, and not already thinking about the next thing. Sometimes we also shared dinners with other travelers, which gave us all a sense of community; a diverse group of people looking for the same thing—enjoying the dinner and watching the sunset.

We met all sorts of travelers on the way: Solo, couples, and families, ranging from short vacations to living in the van for months or years, and everybody seemed to have figured out the ideal way for themselves. This was honestly one of the most interesting parts of my travels; the new perspectives on life one gets by talking to different kinds of people. While at home, we are mostly around the same people, do the same work, talk about the same things, eat the same food, structure the same weekends, and so on. Anything that goes beyond our typical scope of operation we usually perceive as rather unpleasant or even "foreign" to us. Hence, opportunities for new experiences are somewhat limited unless we actively seek them. In all honesty, the "old" me, with his limited views and beliefs, would have viewed many of these people in a negative way. They wouldn't have fit the old ideals I had taken on over the years of studying and working exclusively around the same type of people. How can someone that is totally career focused and trained to work as a machine be open or understanding to the different worldview of just living in a van for maximum freedom and doing some work on the side to get along? Right, they probably cannot. What we would likely do is judge and try to impose our established framework on this other way of life but fail to do so. And then? We would talk it down and find excuses for not having to change anything in our existing, comfortable blueprint of life. Unfortunately, that is how many of us (including me back then) think and operate, often even unconsciously.

Personally, I have learned not to judge anymore, to have little opinions about other peoples' lives (unless it impacts me directly), and to always be open to learning something new regardless of how contrary to my existing belief system it may seem. Isn't that what makes life really exciting in the end? Otherwise, we would just have one monotonous stream of predictable activities that practically makes us relive our past on a daily basis, and that would imply past = future. Maybe that is exactly what many people seek, and there is absolutely nothing wrong with it—a steady state with no upside is valued higher than temporary uncertainty or discomfort with an upside. However, when we honestly look back on our life and evaluate the real big and life-changing events, have these been actively planned, or did they occur by chance? I am sure most of us will agree that the really big and important events just happened and were not (consciously) planned. For me, it was the trigger event in NYC that increased my internal pain level to the maximum and therefore pushed me to quit without a new plan. Otherwise, I would have probably never let go of all my fixed structures, taken so much time off, had all these new experiences, and been here in Portugal living in a van. I think we can perfectly summarize it as follows: Life only really begins where our plans end! And that was also the storyline for many people we met along the way. Were they running from something? Maybe, but as long as they stay honest with themselves and are prepared to find their way back, that is totally fine.

After we had to return the van, J and I decided that we wanted to stay in Portugal for a bit longer to explore the Algarve region in the south. We carefully selected a few locations far into nature. Our first stop was a small campsite in the mountains that offered a handful of tents to rent. There were no other guests when we arrived, and we could fully enjoy the space by ourselves. The kitchen was outdoors, basically an open cooking area. A few hammocks hung between the trees, and a few wooden camping toilets were available to use. The view from the toilet on the mountaintop was honestly impressive, the most peaceful and inspirational setting one could wish for. In addition, the campsite had two loyal dogs, Manny and Chuva. We really loved the two. They were so calm and reliable. Each day we took long exploration walks with them; they would always return after running off for a bit and would wait at each cross-path to see which way we would go. We were friends, a synchronized team consisting of two humans and two dogs.

In the past, I'd never had affection for dogs or animals in general. I had the perspective that "We are humans, they are animals. They are not like us; we don't have a connection to them," which was part of my left-brain-tilted way of living and the corresponding emotional availability that a working robot has. During my travels, that had completely changed. I started feeling a real connection to animals again, not being afraid or wary of them but enjoying the honest companionship these lovely creatures provide. In the rest of the chapter, you will find that each of my next stops had either dogs or other animals as part of the overall happening—coincidence? No! If a new lesson must be learned, circumstances will always align and bring the relevant experiences to us.

One of my favorite moments was when we were on one of our daily walks with Manny and Chuva. At one point, I took a side road through the bushes for a part of the way. Once I returned to the main path, I didn't immediately see J and went back to see if she had fallen behind, but I couldn't find her. When I turned around, Chuva was jumping out of the bushes; Manny was already sitting farther ahead on the path, waiting for us. I thought that J had maybe already gone up to the camp, as we had no water with us, and it was pretty hot, hence I also made my way up. I called Chuva and started walking. After a few steps, I noticed he wouldn't follow. I called again and kept on walking. Again, no sign of Chuva, who would usually follow us closely when we called him. I went back on the way and found him sitting behind the curve, looking at me with big eyes, indicating that something was not right. I felt that he wanted to tell me something and asked, "Is it J? She is not yet on the way back, is she?" He kept looking at me, wagged his tail, and followed me once I started making my back on the path. A few minutes later, we saw J coming toward us, exhausted from the sun, on her way back to the camp. She indeed was not yet in front of me, I had passed her. Chuva ran toward her, licked her legs, and finally reunited us. We thanked, petted, and praised him and marched back together as a team of four. It was possible to communicate with animals after all! A lesson that the young woman we met the next day still had to embark on.

The next day, a new guest arrived. A young woman in her mid-thirties, traveling with a car through Portugal for two weeks. She was pregnant and taking her last time out alone before returning to her new life, which she was not yet fully ready to accept. Even though we communicated quite a bit during the two days of our overlapping stay, there was no sincere connection between us. Do you know that feeling when you see someone and immediately know that you don't like that person for whatever reason? That was the case between us—of course, I made sure not to let the old me be in control any longer, but I could still feel my past patterns trying to come up. However, after I had just learned to be open and accepting toward all people, I would definitely not stop now.

But what exactly was it that she rejected in me and that I didn't like in her? After a day of having to share the kitchen, hammocks, and the small camp space in general, we both figured out what the root of it was. I told her about my story—that I worked in finance in the big cities of this world but then needed more freedom and nature and hence quit my job. She told me about her story; how she is—or used to be—against the system, hating all forms of capitalism and disliking those traditionally successful people, but now had married a doctor and gotten pregnant. Basically, I represented all that she had and still opposed while she embodied a version of life that I would have looked down on just a year before. We both knew it. I could see it in her eyes, and she in mine, but we would not bring such honesty to the table after having just met the other person the day before. Also, we would part ways in only two days, and hence there was no need to cause drama.

On one occasion, both of us sat at the main table in front of the outdoor kitchen, and we talked about the specific circumstances of her traveling alone in pregnancy. I could clearly sense the inner conflict in her, that she was not yet ready to let go of her old identity as the rebellious anti-girl. But she had to! She was pregnant now, rented a small house outside the city with the doctor, and had to become a part of the society she used to condemn so much in the past. She told me that she could not live in the city center any longer because she hated seeing all those seemingly successful people every day. She was also angry about the fact that at home, her sister was apparently the favorite daughter with her straight career track and life in common order. It was obvious why she became so attached to the identity of the angry, hating anti-girl; it was an easy coping mechanism to cover up the feelings of insecurity and insufficiency—probably for years. The emotions of anger and hate popped up regularly during our conversations, and I wondered why she was still so full of both when she was about to become a mother in a few weeks. Then I realized that she was on the right path but simply needed more time. She tried, step by step, to let go of the hurt little girl, becoming the version of herself that she now needed to be. Please don't get me wrong, I am certainly not a perfect person myself; the reason why I am so specific about this part is that I'd had to do the same exercise myself over the last year and hence deeply felt what was happening to her.

I stirred my coffee, took a sip, and put the cup back down. I looked her in the eyes and commenced with the following example in a calm, non-finger-pointing manner: Imagine there is a football match, team white against team blue. Now there are different levels of support you can show for your team, each with its own depths of attachment to the outcome of the actual match. Let us consider three illustrative levels.

Level 1:

You don't really mind who wins the game. You like to be with people, watch the dynamics of the match, maybe have a drink, feel the energy in the stadium, and rumble a few songs together. You see team white scoring, and you cheer. You see team blue scoring, and you cheer. You are not attached to the outcome of the game at all, you are here for the event itself. You joke around with both team white and blue representatives without any repercussions. After the game is over, you go home and enjoy the rest of the day, regardless of who won.

Level 2:

You have supported team white since you were a kid. Your parents and close friends support the same team, and you like to go to the games together. You get euphoric when team white scores, you enjoy the ecstasy of the moment, you feel part of something bigger, a collective of people with the same (temporary) beliefs and goals. Nevertheless, at the same time, you get a little sad when team blue scores and noticeably angry when team blue wins. You don't like it; you want your team to win. You may even throw an empty plastic cup at the section of team blue opponents on your way out of the stadium. For the rest of the day, your emotions are mixed; you can still feel a bit of sadness and anger, but ultimately you let go of it, and the next day everything is fine again. You joke with one of your colleagues, who supports team blue, and go about your regular day. You have a medium level of attachment.

Level 3:

All your friends are team white. You don't even talk to people from team blue. People supporting that team represent something that disgusts you, that you cannot identify with at all, that you condemn to the core. If team blue scores, a strong tension builds up inside you, and if team blue wins, your anger and hate start bursting forth uncontrollably. You may get into verbal and physical fights with team blue representatives, forget your morals, and even become mean or violent. The outcome of the game controls you. For days, for weeks, for years. You are so strongly attached to team white that it has become your identity. Your baseline personality depends on team white's success: You are euphoric when team white wins or full of hate when they lose.

I finished off the example and didn't say anything further. I left room for her to react if she wanted to, but she didn't. She simply acknowledged with a "Mmh." I drank my coffee and then stood up to wash the dishes. That was it. Nothing else needed to be discussed, clarified, or justified at that point. I knew it clicked for her because the same example had also clicked for me sometime earlier. We understood each other. Maybe our superficial differences were actually just a cover-up for our deeper commonalities.

The next day, I sat at the table again to read a book (J took a nap). Manny and Chuva gave me company, under the table in the shade. The young woman came by to make herself a tea and sat down with a book at the table as well. We said hi, had a little small talk, and then continued reading, both for ourselves. After a while, Chuva came out from below the table to get his daily dose of attention—I petted and played around with him a little. Then he walked to the young woman and sat down next to her. She didn't react. He started snarling to make her turn around, but again no reaction. I looked up and saw her face had turned red. Something was boiling inside her—she couldn't open herself up to give him some attention or to briefly pet him. Now Chuva started barking because he seemed to feel that there was a certain tension between them. I wondered what was going on and suggested, "I think he just wants you to pet him a little."

Whereupon she replied, "Dogs are wild creatures for me. I don't touch them," and stood up. Frankly, I was a little shocked, again. How could someone be so cold, especially when a baby was just weeks away? Though I also felt compassion for her. These categorical rejections founded on fear and insecurity also represented what had been "me" in the past. Only over the last year had I really allowed my emotions to become visible, and it definitely was a process. The same process she was in, just at an earlier stage. She simply needed a bit more time.

That day I realized that every person we meet in life is there to teach us a lesson, seemingly good or bad, as they will show us our own weaknesses and trigger points. I learned that I partially still had my old patterns and views anchored somewhere inside me and that I needed to detach from them further. Also, I realized that "I had been her" not too long ago in the sense of being identified with all sorts of external things, and in the sense of emotional coldness that helped to protect my own feelings from getting hurt. Overall, I was happy that we met her; she was a gift that mirrored my old self to me, showed me how far I had already come and what I needed to work on further.

After this insightful campsite experience, J and I moved to another, even more rudimentary, place in the mountains a few hours away. The land was owned by a lady in her mid-sixties who had immigrated to Portugal two years before. She grew a garden, put two furnished camper van shells on the ground (one for her, one to be rented out), and constructed the kitchen in the open stone ruin in the middle of the land. It was great, being totally off-grid, with barely any internet, and living a totally reduced lifestyle. Only the old lady, one other couple (who had moved in with her two months before), and us. We read books, cooked food, chopped some wood, and watered the plants. Each day was so simplistic that every small act became exciting in itself. However, J noted that she would like to go to more developed places from then on, and we agreed to leave one day earlier. She wanted to take a shower in peace, go to a toilet that offered at least a little bit of privacy, and be in an environment that felt not too lonely. While I personally loved these somewhat special experiences, I also understood her view and agreed to leave earlier.

Our next stop was a cottage, a charming and beautiful place with a few big stone rooms, each with its own fireplace, for rent. The place also had two cute dogs, Thelma and Louise, who were always on the property. We loved playing around with them, and they would visit us regularly to sneak a view into our room to check if there might be some food to snatch. We had no car, and the closest small food store was around half an hour's walk away, but we really enjoyed our daily tour to buy fresh cooking ingredients. In the evenings, we would collect firewood from all around the property, prepare and eat dinner, and then light up the fireplace to just sit and enjoy our time together. During those days, and for the first time, I felt a little more than just companionship coming up between us. I knew it was not love but also not just friends. It was something in the middle, and I wanted to open myself to the possibility for potentially more to develop. At least I could try to give whatever we had a chance to evolve into a soft form of relationship. Not forcing anything but allowing things to happen. We were emotionally very close for the last two days, and it was a wonderful end to our trip. A delightful blend of coastal beauty, natural retreats, and historical charm. The day of departure had come—J flew back home, and I stayed for another week in Portugal.

Max Tower

I booked a tent in a somewhat hidden camp in the forests of Portugal. The place was very chaotic yet functioned well, disturbing at first sight yet so welcoming at second glance, and the close interaction between all twenty to thirty people living on the site gave a warm big-family feeling. It was a mix of people specifically looking for camp life, some stranded people temporarily living there who didn't have elsewhere to go, and some who simply stuck around after their initial visit. Maybe one could call it a hippie camp, but with a less forced way of life. Ages varied between twenty to sixty years, but predominantly young people. Some were living in simple tents, some in trailers or campers, and some even built their own wooden houses. A chaotic mix with a harmonic community. After the first day, I had already connected with most people. Nobody judged any other (at least not publicly), and everybody was open to talking—about life, their camp experiences, and what brought them here. Rarely have I seen a place where such a diverse group of people comes together yet gets along so well. Everybody was so peaceful, simply relaxed, without any pressure. While I wanted to stay fit and took the daily walk to the supermarket through the forest, around one hour each way, others took the community car and bought food and water for everyone who put their items on the common shopping list. It was a well-functioning organization with very few rules and a maximum focus on freedom—everybody could do whatever they wanted; the area was big enough.

During the day, we talked, cooked, played ball sports, frisbee, table tennis, or simply relaxed. In the evenings, many of us would sit together and have a few drinks, play instruments, and enjoy the community. Honestly, the energy I felt during those nights was quite unique, like a magic bond between everybody participating (actively or passively) in the group. We all got along. Some gathered around the table exchanging stories and views, some were just quietly by themselves on the sofas yet in proximity to the rest, and some sat outside playing guitar and wooden drums. People would switch locations during the night, some went to sleep, and some others joined, but nothing could destroy the positive, welcoming atmosphere of the group. I loved that place! I understood why so many people simply stuck around much longer after their initial visit—the place had its own way of making you feel connected, home, and unconditionally accepted. Everything just flowed naturally; there was no forced theme or agenda. The overall vibe was a wonderful mix of everyone's individual notes. On my last day, I was actually thinking of extending my stay but ultimately decided to go home. It was time to spend some time with family again, especially to see how my dad was doing.

Back at home, the summer was in full force, and we all gathered for my dad's birthday in mid-July. We met for coffee and cake and spent a peaceful afternoon in the garden together. In addition, he scheduled a dinner with a small group of ten people for later that day. That was the evening he was so eagerly working toward in the months before, I presume. Unfortunately, he was not feeling very strong that day but still pushed himself to the planned dinner. We could clearly see that he was struggling, but it was important to him; it was the last birthday he would celebrate, and he knew that. I am very happy that he was able to be with everyone one more time exactly on his birthday—it was his way of saying thank you and probably an early goodbye to all of us. The following days he seemed a bit better, somewhat relieved from the uncertainty and pressure of the dinner night. We spent a few more heartfelt afternoons in the sun together and talked about our wonderful childhood time—my sister and I were not short of stories and anecdotes: How he taught us swimming and cycling, how he showed us what persistence and discipline mean, how he was always there for us even when we caused trouble, and how he helped us move when we went to university. It was an emotional time that helped us all to partially let go before the unavoidable event happened. We knew that by now it was a matter of weeks. We discussed what we should do, and what he did not want was that we would just sit at home in grief, basically waiting for "the day". That would have had a very sad character to it and put a certain pressure or expectation on him as well. We all agreed that we should continue the way we did before, and if anything happened, we would immediately come home.

During my days at home, I remembered my encounter with the mysterious Danish guy on the bus on the way to the Sahara. He had told me about the workaway concept, where one is provided with shelter and food in exchange for a few hours of work per day. It sounded very interesting to me, but to date, I had never tried it because, after all, I had worked for several years and therefore had available savings. However, I knew a place where the workaway concept would be an ideal fit: Norway. It was perfect to combine work in nature with actual farm experience. I set up an account, sent out two applications, and three days later organized my first two-week workaway experience near Ålesund, Norway.

It was a small, beautiful farm owned by a young, modern family. The mother and father were in their early forties, and the three kids were between eight to fourteen years old. Besides me, a young woman in her mid-twenties had arrived the day before and would stay for three weeks. She was very friendly and companionable, and we got along well the whole time—we shared the "volunteer floor" downstairs with its own bathroom and eating area. Also, everyone had their own bedroom, which is not always a given in the different workaway setups around the world. The family was very welcoming and made us feel relaxed and at home from day one. While we were there to work and learn new things, they also put great effort into making sure we would have a good and enjoyable time.

We did quite a bit of fieldwork the first few days. For example, we hand-weeded most of the area, planted new salad greens, thinned out the carrots field, dug out potatoes, picked raspberries, and prepared veggie boxes to be sold at the weekly farmer's market. It was a good way to train our leg and back muscles and to further get to know each other. She had just come out of a breakup with her girlfriend, needed a break from everything at home, and hence came to Norway to clear her mind. She still seemed a bit hurt and confused, but overall did very well. On the first night, we sat together in the volunteer eating area and shared a cup of tea, talked about her and my way to this farm, and simply gave each other company. I offered her a few comforting words that she probably needed to hear—that she did the right thing, that it is okay to feel sad for a while, that there is nothing to worry about, that the confusion will transform into new energy soon, and that life is a path full of decisions which ultimately work in our favor. I decided to lend her one of my books—that would hopefully help her to see things from a different perspective—to read over the coming days. I myself had just borrowed it a few months earlier from one of the public bookshelves in Austria.

"Try to feel what you read, not to only comprehend it with your mind," I said and added, "For me, this book only worked once I was ready for it. The first time in 2019, nothing really clicked as I could not grasp the basic underlying concepts of, e.g., ego versus consciousness; this was all too far away for me back then. The second time in 2022, I found the book again (or it found me) at the right time, and then I was internally ready to not only understand but also feel what it was about. Then it clicked, and the book became a real gem." She thanked me, we drank our tea, and went to bed for the night. In the following days, she would indeed read the book, and we also discussed some of the concepts over breakfast, lunch, or work. It felt right to pass on the "good" that had also come to me over the last year, to help other people on their way to liberation as well, to be simply available for discussions while not forcing my own opinion on them. This was a recurring thing I noticed multiple times during my travels: Supporting other people gave me the satisfaction and purpose that my old finance job no longer could.

Every day I took one of the three Greenland dogs for a run, in iterations. This breed is very powerful, usually bigger than

Two Years

huskies, and needs a lot of activity. I really liked to take them with me—or rather them taking me—as it forced me to stay active. Given it was summer, they could not pull the sleds they were used to pulling in the winter, and hence warmly welcomed any alternative. One day, I had just opened the door of their big cage for the regular clean-up. Milo (the biggest of them) took the opportunity to sneak through my legs out of the enclosure. He jumped around so happily, being free and not on the leash, just having duped this naïve German volunteer. Then he spotted the little baby goat eating grass: He leaped over the fence, positioned in front of the goat, stared at it for a few seconds, and suddenly ran off again. I tried to catch him but of course had no success. He had reached the street by now, rushing from tree to tree, leaving his pee marks. Thankfully, the other volunteer got the smart idea to shake his food can. He finished his business, turned around, located the shaking sounds, and immediately ran back to the farm. I ran after him and saw the young woman lying on the ground (he simply ran over her) and the oldest son holding Milo by the collar. I thanked both of them and put him back in the enclosure. What a relief. I was genuinely happy that Milo didn't attack the baby goat that day because, after all, he still had remaining bits of wolf character and instinct in him. When we shared the story at dinner, everyone was surprised that Milo really didn't attack. Usually, he as well as the others would do so—they regularly caught goats or chickens coming too close. From that day on, I made absolutely sure none of them would ever escape again, while keeping my routine of taking them on runs and walks with me.

For the next few days, I mainly worked with the father in the mountainous part of their land. We hammered fence poles into the ground around the whole area, up and down the hill. He would go first, paving the way by cutting the bushes. I would go after him, carrying the poles on my back and manually hammering them in. It was a great exercise for the whole body, and we worked well together as a team. It felt good to do some real physical work—something I hadn't done in a very long time, probably more than a decade. It was a different feeling of fulfillment to see something that you have built yourself grow. It was different in the sense that we built it for ourselves, not for somebody else. An important factor for motivation. Maybe in the future, I should try to create something on my own rather than being employed by somebody else.

After work, we had free time to go on hikes in the mountains surrounding the valley, bike around the area, go to the nearby lake to swim and fish, or to simply enjoy our free time on the farm. I loved to visit the two Fjord horses in the afternoons. They lived in their huge land area in the mountains and were happy for anyone to come by to visit them. It was so calm and rewarding just to be around them. Exactly what I needed after a long day of physical work. In the evenings, mostly the father would cook; he loved it and was really good at it. While breakfast and lunch were separate, dinner was a whole family activity. It felt great to share a good meal, exchange stories, and occasionally have a drink together—we were practically part of the family the whole time. On my last day, I had a more personal conversation with the mother about how they came to buy the farm and if they had any future plans for it. She

Two Years

explained that it was the most exciting thing to buy that land with the old property, to rebuild everything, and to bring things up and running again. Though now that everything was stable, she admitted to feeling a little "stuck" on the farm. Each day was practically the same, not much else to look forward to. I felt what she said because I had been in a comparable situation just a year before, but I never had kids to take care of that limited my flexibility. Over the coming days, I spent a while thinking about a potential scenario of me owning a farm and living that life long-term but concluded that it wouldn't be something for me at this time in my life. Not before I could feel more comfortable with having experienced many more ways of living, many more countries and cultures, and much more time with myself to figure out what it was that I really wanted.

The next stop was a combination of farm and camp in the northern part of the country. It was located directly at a fjord and therefore attracted many hobby fishers. The family had two young boys, four and nine years old, and additionally took care of underprivileged children from around the area. The animals on this site comprised two horses, many goats and chickens, and eleven huskies. They were not as huge as the Greenland dogs but at least similarly active and endurant. Besides me, there was another young woman in her early twenties volunteering. We slept in trailers on the campground and had our own separate outdoor kitchen, which we shared with the other guests at the campsite. The setup and vibe were a bit different compared to the previous place, a little more distant. Not the feeling of "you are one of us" but rather "you are the volunteers visiting us"—which was totally fine as there are many different ways to approach this.

Breakfast and lunch we ate separately (volunteers had to bake their own bread), and dinner we all shared together each night. We cooked in rotations and thereby had the opportunity to taste all varieties of food and cooking skills, ranging from bad to acceptable. Frankly, none of us did a really good job at cooking, but everyone took it with humor. After dinner, we usually played a few board games with the kids and then went back to our trailers. The work was comparable to the previous farm: I helped with the renovation work on one of the houses, took on various one-off tasks on the campsite where needed, stacked the firewood in the cellar, and one day even cleaned the barn—which was full of dry shit crusted on the floor, ceiling, and walls—by hand with a high-pressure cleaner. Each task I took on with a smile because that was what I had signed up for, and frankly, it was also fun to push through those rather unpleasant things, such as the barn: My face and jacket were covered in shit that flaked off the floor, ceiling, and walls. I tasted it, I smelled it, and I touched it. But I kept growling my motivational songs, nevertheless. What else was there to do, right? Acceptance is what I had learned earlier that year in the desert; now was the time to apply it in practice.

The huskies became my friends in no time. At first, one has no idea how to distinguish them, but after a few days, one gets to know the fine details in appearance and, more importantly, the differences in character. Each one of them had their own style, like within a big group of humans. Sometimes I would take them on walks individually to get to know them better and to give them an opportunity to get out of the known farm environment. In addition, we would let them freely run in their big compound for a few hours each day. It was mainly my task to watch them and make sure that nothing would happen while they were playing. Honestly, it was such a great and rewarding feeling to become one of their pack, playing and running around with them while also being respected for commands.

Among them were two sisters who used to get along well in the past but then got separated for a while and reunited later, from which point onward, they simply could not stand each other any longer. I don't know what exactly had happened during that time, but now there was uneven competition between them. One took on the role of the perpetrator, and the other the role of the victim. When all of them were playing in the compound together, usually the perpetrator would initiate some form of "hunt" on her sister, and some of the others would join in so that in the end, there was a group of five or more huskies circling around the victim. The temporary solution was to leash the perpetrator to the fence so that she could still move and run around, just in a smaller radius. In addition, she was usually the last one to be guided from her kennel into the playing field and back.

At some point, I wanted to try a different method as it appeared the temporary solutions that had been applied so far weren't very effective. I would not leash the perpetrator to the fence but follow her closely throughout the compound instead. Every time she attempted an "attack" on her sister, I would interfere and chase her off. She tried a few times, but I didn't let her get what she wanted. The attempts became less frequent over the hours, and the other dogs also seemed to sense that this was not the time to circle the victim anymore—they mostly left her alone. At the end, I took the perpetrator out a few minutes earlier than the others; she had to understand that if she wouldn't stop attacking her sister, she would not get to play with the rest of the pack. One by one, I then also led the others back to their kennels. The next day, when it was their playing time, I repeated the same method. Before I led the perpetrator to the compound, I kneeled down, firmly held her neck, looked her in the eyes, and shook my head. She knew exactly what this meant. No words were needed. She remembered from the previous day.

In the compound, she behaved surprisingly well. No real attempts to chase after or attack her sister anymore, rather an avoidance of close contact, or, if getting close by accident, not becoming aggressive. This was so satisfying to see. Finally, the victim could move freely without being chased around all the time. In the beginning, she ran up to me for protection a few times, but that became less frequent. In the end, I didn't even need to chase anyone off anymore. She was confident enough to act on her own. The following situation nicely illustrates how fast things had changed within just two days: In the beginning, the victim would always run and hide under the big bench in the middle of the field. Her sister and the other dogs would jump on top and circle around it until they let up, and she could come out. Where do you think the victim took a seat after those two days? Exactly, on top of the bench! On top, where before her sister or the other dogs would sit, bullying her. Now she felt confident enough to repeatedly jump on it

Two Years

and enjoy a new perspective from that position. When the two crossed each other on the field, I could observe that the contacts became at least a bit more friendly, even though they wouldn't play together or trust each other yet. The last change I made was to leave both of them until the end in the compound instead of taking the victim out first and the perpetrator last. I wanted to see how they would behave when being just by themselves. Logically, they wouldn't really interact with each other during that time; it was too early for that. I tried to animate both to play catching sticks with me, but only one of them would consent to play while the other would do her own thing. However, at least there were short moments of intersection where the two briefly smelled each other before running off in their respective directions again. This was a very wholesome development over just a few days; the overall process would take more time, though. I don't know how the two sisters have been doing since I left, but I sincerely hope they became closer again. After all, they were still sisters and part of the same pack with the same goal: To pull the sled as fast as possible.

It was mid-August by now, and my dad's situation got worse. He had become very sick, spending most of the day in bed or on the sofa. Too weak to take walks outside. Barely eating anything. It could have been one of those typical "down phases" that usually lasted a few days but then would pass. But we felt that this time was different. He didn't even want to talk to us on the phone anymore, partially due to his weakness but probably also his fear and discomfort of saying goodbye on the phone. We knew what we had to do and booked our flights home. Luckily, his wife took care of him at home during all this time—he was never alone and never needed an external caregiver. She did a wonderful job, and he was very happy with her being at his side. Hence, we could all sit around his bed and be at home with him for his last few days—the dying process. I don't want to go into details of what such a process typically looks like, but just imagine the body won't be given any more food or water and will thereby naturally find its way to death, with the help of heavy painkillers, of course. We held his hand, we sang songs for him, we cried, we sat in silence, and we helped him lie comfortably. Either alone, just my sister and me, or as a group; we rotated and made sure each one of us had enough time with him. Enough time to let him know everything he needed to know, enough time to say goodbye, enough time to let go, enough time to comprehend the situation. Even though he was not visibly conscious any longer, he would react back when we pressed his hand. Or he would try to open his eyelids when we played guitar and sang his favorite song. He knew he wasn't alone; he knew we were there with him. And that was the most important thing. We love you, Dad!

This was a very emotional experience for all of us, of an intensity that I had never experienced before. However, I am very happy that we all could be with him on his "way back", and that we'd had enough time to prepare for the day over the previous months. I can imagine the shock of a sudden or unexpected death is magnitudes harder. The whole experience also took away the fear of death to a certain degree, and that is probably something we all have to fight with regularly during our lifetime, often acting it out unconsciously. In my opinion: The more we identify with our ego-self, the higher the fear of mortality and death, and vice versa. Does only the physical body die? How will the essence of consciousness make its way back, and where to? Will the purpose of life be revealed at that specific point? Does the soul reincarnate? We all have to face these kinds of questions at some point, and from my perspective, one should believe whatever suits them best to prepare for the "way back".

Over the next days, I further reflected on the last years of my life. What, really, was the purpose of life? It surely couldn't be just extensive pleasure hunts—I had ruled that out with certainty by now. It also couldn't be just the standard blueprint of working, having a family, and going on until "day X" without asking deeper questions. It somehow had to also involve the rediscovery of our true essence, the privilege of experiencing who or what we really are at the core. I decided that going forward, I would put even greater emphasis on passing on what I was lucky enough to learn over the last year, helping other people on their way to liberation. But was that really it? Was it my purpose to selectively pass on bits of knowledge wherever possible? Shouldn't there be more structure to it? Even though I couldn't specifically pin it down yet, I knew that I was getting closer. But for now, I needed a few days' rest at home with my family.

Quest for Love

We spent the next days together as a family, and each of us took the necessary time to mourn our dad's death. As we had enough time to mentally prepare and properly say goodbye, it was a bit easier for us to accept the situation and let him go in peace. J and I spoke about what had happened (she already knew the day would come before long), and I told her that I was thinking about making my long-envisaged Asia trip soon, in line with my dad's reflection during one of our last conversations. "I wish I would have spent more time exploring the world. I know I have seen quite a bit and shouldn't complain, but there are so many more places, cultures, and lifestyles that I will never get the chance to understand or experience now. You and your sister are doing the right thing—take your necessary time and make sure to keep those memories safe." We agreed to meet in Bali, Indonesia, in early September.

Max Tower

The island Is a beautiful place characterized by tradition, quietness, and nature in the middle and northern parts but also lots of gentrification and tourism, especially in the southern part. In the hot spots of the island, such as Ubud, Canggu, or Kuta, the atmosphere was rather dense and solely tailored to tourism. It has basically become a Western world, just in a more tropical climate. Little is left of the original Balinese culture as foreigners have taken over the area: Shops and restaurants are predominantly owned by expats, prices have risen to Western standards, and digital nomads are flooding the island trying to find their (temporary) new homes. A very busy place geared toward profit maximization. The less frequented places, on the other hand, offer a unique mix of scenic elegance and cultural richness: Lush green landscapes as far as the eye can see, with terraced rice paddies cascading down the hills and swaying palm trees lining land and beaches. Many temples stand as majestic reminders of traditional Balinese heritage; the chanting and bellringing during ceremonies create a sense of serenity and sacredness. Frangipani and other tropical plants enrich the air with a floral sweetness.

J's and my relationship was still more on the friends side, but after our wonderful trip to Portugal a few months ago—especially the last stop at the cottage—I wanted to remain open to all possibilities. It was easy between us, and we got along so well. We almost never fought, and we always agreed on activities, food, and the next destinations very smoothly. There was no intention on my side of changing her as a friend at all; she was perfect as she was. However, when I tried to see her from the viewpoint of a potential long-term partner, I noticed that I started to judge her and found more and more things that I wanted to change in her—her appearance as well as character-wise. And that was not a good basis to start with; real love should be somewhat unconditional, not overly focused on the negative aspects, and should come from the heart rather than the mind.

We tried. We continued our friends-with-benefits model but added more tenderness in the form of hugging, stroking, and kissing each other more frequently. It felt okay, but unfortunately never passed that level. I really would have loved for it to be something more, but it simply wasn't. Love cannot be forced. After all that we went through together, it would have been such a beautiful story between us: Two people looking for the same thing, freedom and travel, finding each other, going through tough times together, yet coming out stronger as a couple. But that was it—only a great story; our (mostly my) emotions were not real. In addition, I felt that our views on life started to diverge. While I spent increasingly more time on spiritual topics as part of my self-development, J was not really passionate about those things. She also visited the temples sometimes but was not seeking to expand her mind and worldview on a deeper level. I tried to have more complex and philosophical conversations about life with her occasionally, but unfortunately, it never was as fruitful as I had hoped. We simply didn't share the same interests and beliefs any longer, and that was okay. Sometimes we change, and not always can our counterpart make that change with us.

Our remaining time together was great, nevertheless. We continued to explore the rest of the island in small intervals on our scooter and enjoyed the variety of Balinese food options such as Ayam Pelalah, Nasi Campur, and Nasi/Mie Goreng with all their fusions of flavor to the fullest; like in many Asian countries, the authentic, traditional food is served quite spicy. After all, we had shared something special over the last year; it just wasn't love. It was a valuable friendship. We were grateful for our time together and appreciated everything that had happened—we both grew a lot during that period, each in our own way. At the end of September, J had to fly back home as she would start her new job soon; we parted on good terms and are still in occasional contact today. I stayed for a week longer, got food poisoning (the famous Bali belly), and finally departed to my next destination, Vietnam, the first week of October.

Late at night, I landed in Hanoi, where I stayed in the exuberant and lively Old Quarter of the city. I immediately fell in love with its atmosphere: So many different little shops, tiny street restaurants, and traditional businesses to explore. The first three days were simply exciting—all I had to do was walk around the narrow, curvy streets and let the impressions work on me. Become one with the chaos. Merge with the happenings. It felt like stepping back in time; the most ancient part of Hanoi had preserved much of its traditional charm. Especially the culinary street food offerings made it a vibrant and lasting experience. All variations of Pho were my absolute favorite, and I would usually eat it twice per day. A symphony of background noises, clearly dominated by the horns of motorbikes weaving through the streets, rounded the overall experience off. While the traffic in Vietnam is among the most crowded

Two Years

and intense I have seen throughout the years, the diverse and impressive character of the Old Quarter more than made up for it. One night I visited Beer Street (a small street right in the center, packed with bars and clubs) for the first time and felt an urge to join the party crowd coming up in me. In the prior months, I had been mainly focused on myself and my inner world, but now I wanted to get in touch with people in the outer world again and enjoy the nightlife in Vietnam. Additionally, I found Vietnamese women among the most stunning I have encountered so far in the world; I was fascinated by their unique combination of traditional values, kindness, and beauty in equal parts. Even though I had never been in love with J, we basically stayed exclusive during our time together—I wanted to be a good person and do the right thing after what had happened in New York between my ex-girlfriend and me. However, here in Hanoi, I ultimately felt that it was time to let go, move on, and give in to the upcoming urge of needs. I knew that partying or chasing women wouldn't be a solution for anything, but I had to follow my instincts. It was time to live a little, and who knew, maybe I would find even more than just physical pleasure along the way.

The events in this small street were always exciting. Each night I would try out different bars or clubs and meet a ton of new people, locals as well as tourists. The synergy of the small available space and the sheer number of people looking for the same thing made the nights so ecstatic. It was great to let the "old" me out for a bit, it was exactly what I needed for a change: Indulge in pleasure. While it was actually not really my thing anymore, as I enjoyed silent and insightful nights by myself or with selected people much more, at this point, I had to give in, release self-control, and live out all unfulfilled needs, for something better to come. Today, I know that I had to do it exactly that way in order to reach my "I am done" point, from which onward, I was ready to open myself up for something more meaningful. A few nights out, dates, and hollow one-night stands later, I matched with C on one of the typical dating apps. We met, and I was immediately (but prematurely) blown away by her. She was so cute, so polite, so shy, but at the same time so hot, flawlessly shaped, and good-looking. A great combination that one could colloquially call "wife material". She seemed perfect.

Over the hours of our first date, I felt how strongly I was attracted to her both physically and character-wise. I just wanted to hold her in my arms all the time, hold her hand, kiss her, take care of her, protect her. A feeling that I hadn't had for a very long time. Was it just the excitement of the latest new thing? Or was there indeed something deeper coming up inside me? But so fast? How was that possible? After the night out, I took her to a taxi and also went home myself. Even though I found her extremely attractive, I didn't mind taking it a bit slower as I saw more in her than just another. She also enjoyed our time together a lot, and hence we decided to meet again the next day.

Our second day together was equally great as the first, but this time I told her that I would leave Hanoi soon for a few days to explore other areas of the country in nature. We had also talked about how long I expected to stay in Hanoi on the previous day, but not in such detail that I could give a concrete time frame. After all, I was somewhat flexible and would have stayed longer to get to know her better if we both had felt this was something real. When I actually mentioned leaving Hanoi for a few days, she realized that I probably wouldn't be here "forever" and became, justifiably, a bit more defensive. She was not looking for something casual. Me, I was not sure what exactly I was looking for. But every time I saw her, I wanted her to be much more than just another woman. I wanted to be romantic and caring with her, not only sexual. Something I had never felt in the last year—this was different. Something more. Something deeper. Something happening so fast!

I decided that I should go to my planned next stop regardless. The weekend was over, and she had to work during the week. It would have been an odd setup of me waiting for her to finish work to then (potentially) meet afterward, if time allowed. I had been in Hanoi for quite a while now and didn't want to just sit around all day waiting. If our first contact could not survive even a few days' separation, then it probably was never meant to be. Also, my next destination was just three driving hours away. We kept in touch while I was gone and envisaged meeting upon my return to Hanoi. On the second day, there was some misunderstanding during our texting. It came across as if she was just seeing me as some form of entertainment or distraction from a bad experience she had had a few weeks before. In that moment, I honestly felt a little hurt. That beautiful woman that I liked so much suddenly behaved totally differently. Was she just one of "those" after all? My ego, or the little boy in me, actually felt messed around with and hence reacted in the typical way immature men usually react, i.e., being despicable or rude in order to protect their own feelings first. Of course, from her perspective, I was the one behaving incorrectly and hurting her first. The classic chicken and egg situation. What followed was a bit of back and forth, but we solved the misunderstanding and confirmed we'd meet when I was back. We wanted to see each other again. I enjoyed the remaining days in nature and then took the bus back to the city.

On the day we were supposed to meet, she texted me to cancel our date. I was shocked—after we had just solved the misunderstanding, openly talked about how we felt toward each other, and agreed that we wanted to meet, she simply texted me to cancel as if it meant nothing to her. I mainly came back to Hanoi to see her again, to find out if this thing between us had any substance. How could she send me such a plain, unapologetic text, not even showing the slightest sign of regret? Here I was again, hurt by that beautiful young woman that I was so attracted to. My reaction was the same as just a few days before, rough and more direct in tone. I accused her of not knowing what she wanted and not being as much interested in me as I was in her. This time we didn't solve the (cultural) misunderstanding but instead kept silent for a few days. She saw in me the rude guy not being attentive to her feelings, while I saw in her the rude woman not being attentive to mine. I spent the next two days thinking about the situation and whether I had really misunderstood her so many times, but I concluded to myself that she just didn't see me the same way I saw her. She probably thought I was just another tourist looking for some fun in Vietnam, and she was not totally wrong about that. However, my intentions with her were sincere. I told her many times, but her prior bad experience and her general insecurity toward men made this a very difficult situation to win. I tried to comfort her but she wouldn't really believe me. And to be honest, her doubts had every right to exist. Would I have really stayed in Hanoi for much longer just to be with her? Would I be seriously willing to move here? Or was it partially simply the hunting instinct in me that wanted to crack that case? Probably it was a mix of both, driven by this exciting cocktail of emotions I felt for her.

I texted her one last time to ask for a clarifying conversation in person so that we could avoid any potential misunderstandings, but she wasn't interested in meeting. I finally wrote it off, took the few days of pain, and distracted myself with some more nights out in the bars and clubs. I was honestly missing her and wished there was another chance, but I had to accept the situation. Such is life. Not everyone likes you the same way you like them. After a little more reflection, I realized that I was too eager to control the whole situation with her. I wanted it to work so badly that the natural flow got lost, and it became a rather forced opportunity that led me to certainly not behave my best. I told myself that the next time I met someone like her, I would be less attached to the outcome and trust more in the process instead. The encounter with C was a good thing, though; it made me realize that there are indeed strong emotions inside me waiting for the right opportunity to present themselves in the form of love. I was slowly opening myself up to the possibility of finding "the one" on my journey around the world. Why does it always have to be someone from the same school, university, city, or even country? Why should there not be a chance to find something unique somewhere else on the planet? Wouldn't the chance of finding the perfect match be even higher from a global perspective? A way of thinking that I would have completely dismissed just a year earlier because "it would make no sense". But by now, I had become much more open to all kinds of scenarios; I saw possibilities where I had seen sheer impossibility before. I was ready to give it a try. I was willing to act from my heart instead of my mind.

My feelings were mixed during the remaining weeks in Vietnam. On the one hand, I felt that I was looking for something more meaningful, but on the other hand, I didn't feel fully satisfied regarding all my desires yet. I hadn't reached my "I am done" point yet. I knew it was dangerous to fully give in and to indulge in pleasure of all sorts—an easy way to lose oneself, to get carried away by cheap dopamine kicks. Nevertheless, I also knew that I could trust myself enough to cut the line if and when needed, as I had always managed to do so in the past. Anyway, that was all theoretical thinking for now. First, I had to move on from Vietnam, a slightly painful but also eye-opening period for me. I thought about which country could provide a welcoming contrast to Vietnam and swiftly decided on Nepal, the astonishing country surrounded by the Himalayas with eight of the world's ten highest peaks.

Toward the end of November, I landed in Kathmandu, the capital of Nepal. The look and environment of the city and people reminded me of Indian culture (with many small differences); it was somewhat comforting to feel familiar with the way of life here, given my internship in Mumbai ten years ago. The first few days I spent enjoying the city—walking around to explore the beautiful architecture, observing the culture of the locals, and trying the tasty traditional Nepalese cuisine. Especially the Newari food variations, including Samay Baji and Chatamari, I ate regularly; each time, it was such a rich and distinct taste experience thanks to all the thinkable variations thereof. Besides that, Momo and Thukpa were always welcome snacks at any time of the day. Overall, my "landing" in this new country and culture was very similar to how I also approached the Old Quarter of Hanoi a few weeks prior. That was the travel style I had developed over the last few months: First landing in one of the big cities, spending a few days there to get accustomed to the people and culture, and from there, making my way into nature where I could soak in the mesmerizing variety of landscapes away from busy crowds and groups of tourists. Although, I perceived the number of tourists in Nepal as generally less compared to the more popular East Asian countries. It was a welcome change.

Once the initial bliss and excitement of the new impressions settled, I once again (voluntarily) fell back into the pleasure trap. There were a few bars and clubs around, and I felt the need to go out and join the crowd. It was so much fun at the time. Not only experiencing the culture during the day but also at night. Despite the rather strict traditions and a strong focus on family, with partially arranged marriages (I will come to an example later), Nepalese people know how to party quite well. The country is in its decade of change: The current generation of twenty- to thirty-year-olds is right in the middle of tradition versus modernity. Some families have already adapted to the Western way of life, while others still put a strong emphasis on their traditions. Each one of them has to fight for their rights and freedom within the family—some have it easier, some have it harder, and some still simply accept what their parents demand.

With my going-out routine, my desire for the women of the country also began to emerge—not as strongly as in Vietnam, but still noticeable. Consequently, I played around with the typical apps again and set up a few dates. I was once again driven by the lowest forms of pleasures, but I willfully let them drive me; I was conscious of it. I knew what I was doing. I knew I was indulging in pleasure. I knew this was not what I needed in the long term. But I also knew that I had to do it because I was not done yet. I hadn't reached my natural point of satisfaction yet, from where on the need for pleasure would fall off me automatically, without any force. Consequently, I initiated my usual procedures and met a few beautiful Nepalese women. It was fun. It was exciting. And it was distracting. However, what I noticed this time was something different: I did not even get the typical level of dopamine rush out of the mostly meaningless one-night stands any longer. The high from the reward moments became less fierce, and all that was eventually left was a form of physical routine. Like a machine that fulfills a job without any emotions attached to it. What had been so exciting over all the months before suddenly lost its appeal—it seemed that I had potentially (and hopefully) reached my natural point of satisfaction and fulfillment. It was a good first sign, but I wasn't fully convinced yet. Only time would tell.

Next, I booked a room in a small house in the mountains surrounding Kathmandu. It was great to be in silence again, just nature and me, no haunting sound orchestra from motorcycles and cars, and more importantly, no distractions from pleasure traps of all sorts. The view from the mountain was unique: One could clearly see the Himalayas not far away, and especially during sunrise, those moments were extremely peaceful. It was the perfect place to unwind and get back to reading and meditating again, something I had not done much over the last three months. I seemed to always be around people, somewhat busy, but that was what I had wanted at the time, and hence couldn't blame anyone other than myself. Also, those phases of integration were important to not lose touch with the actual human experience. After my deep and transformational months earlier that year, it was time for a period of simply living again. Interestingly, that living time happened to be exactly during my Asia trip, despite being physically and mentally so close to the roots of Buddhism. Though the circumstances brought me to other experiences, and I took them as they came. After all, everything happens for a reason.

On the second day, I woke up and just kept lying in bed. I didn't feel the urge to go out and explore the area, as I would often do. I just kept lying in silence, observing my thoughts passing by, listening to the birds outside, and being totally calm without any agenda or plans. Naturally, the thoughts became fewer and fewer; I didn't put any labels or judgments on them but rather acknowledged them until they finally stopped. I reached the void. A point where there is no thinking, no desire, and no needing. Not even feeling. Just nothingness. An indescribable, natural state of pure awareness or consciousness. It is not forced in the sense of "Now I should feel this and that way to be in peaceful meditation," but rather occurs naturally as a result of letting go of everything and fully embracing the infinity of nothing and everything at the same time. After so many weeks of giving in to desires and distractions, I finally could spend some time as the "real" me again, which I had only rediscovered earlier that year in Austria. This void state was something different from what I had experienced during my previous meditations. It was purer and deeper. It was literally nothing—the ego was completely shut off for several hours. Just simple presence in the eternal black space, yet so comforting and peaceful. It was so much realer than any party, sex, or drug in the material world could ever offer to be, and it was free! It was a needed reminder that I certainly hadn't reached my potential yet with my previous meditations and that there was so much more to understand and explore in the inner world. Everything comes at the right time, always. Sometimes certain events must happen first before we are ready to experience what we are actually meant to see or feel. I was super grateful for this experience, journaled about it, and around noon finally got up and went for lunch.

My next stop was with a local family who rented out a room in their house where I could once again become part of the team for a few days. The family included two daughters in their early and late twenties and their parents. The older daughter just got engaged before I arrived, and everyone was happy and excited for her. It was an arranged marriage. Her parents picked her husband-to-be, and she saw him in person for the first time when he came to town to visit her. Before that, the two had spoken only occasionally on the phone because he lived in the US (he was Nepalese also but had left the country for study and work a few years prior). She seemed okay with it and didn't question the whole situation too much, as it was still a common way to find a future husband or wife in the more rural areas of the country. I knew the concept from my time in India and hence wasn't shocked or anything; I simply acknowledged and was happy together with them. Like in India, many Nepalese people speak a sufficient level of English, and thus we could easily communicate with each other. We joked around about the different cultural approaches to love and life, enjoyed our breakfasts and dinners together, and had a few fun hikes through the mountains. There were more than a handful of monasteries in the area, and hence the mountaintops were vastly covered in colorful pilgrim flags, painting a picture of spiritual significance comparable to a movie scene. Such beautiful scenery and positive energy all around. While a few months before I would have sought more "extreme" activity, in the sense of multiple-day hiking tours, for example, now I just wanted to partake in daily life and become one with the people of the country. To live with them, to eat their food, and to understand their culture. Of course, that was not always easily possible within just a few weeks, but nevertheless, I felt at home very quickly in each place I stayed. It was frankly my favorite way to travel, to live among the people instead of just visiting as a tourist. It was the most real, honest, and heartwarming experience one could ever wish for. In each country, in each culture, in each family. My last stop was at another small family-owned house farther up the mountain, where I had more opportunity to get to know the village people and to enjoy the home-cooked Nepalese cuisine, this time exclusively vegetarian with organically grown ingredients from their own garden. I loved it. During the day, we shucked the corn, collected firewood, and watered the plants, and at night, we sat around the warming campfire together. A perfect environment to end my trip to Nepal. Around mid-December, I flew home for Christmas.

Christmas was a great period for being home. I had missed the European climate after the last three months in Asia. It was great to be back in the known chilly environment and to spend the holidays with family. I also reflected on the last months of travel, everything that had happened, and every place I had been to. I began to realize that I had basically seen the whole world by now—only South America (and Antarctica as a more exotic destination) was missing from the continents, but I did not really have it on my radar until that point. It felt a bit surreal but also impressive that I went around all those places without even having planned any of it. It just happened, one step at a time. By letting go of my old structures, plans, and commitments, a completely new world opened up for me. A beautiful story has been unfolding right in front of my eyes ever since.

I had been free from work for one and a half years by that time. Most of us would probably say that is a very long time. However, for me, that period had passed at lightning speed.

Two Years

After a bit more thinking, I decided that I should do the Central and South America trip as well, now that I had already come so far. If not now, then when? There was no argument against it. In addition, it would put me around the two-year mark of total off-time, which was a psychological threshold I didn't want to cross significantly. At some point, one has to be honest with oneself and acknowledge when enough is enough, or when traveling becomes an escape from reality. Or, in the worst case, when one gets addicted to or even identified with traveling, in the same way I used to be identified with my role as a banker in the past. That was a mistake I did not want to repeat, simply in a different setting. When you are on the road for such a long time, you will automatically meet many types of people who didn't make their exit on time and hence stayed in between the worlds. Some of them were genuinely happy with that, no doubt. But some others were clearly trapped in this middle state and didn't know what to do or where to go. What had started as an exciting journey for them ended in a sad non-belongingness during the search for whatever. I think it was mostly love that most people were missing. Love for themselves and love for and from others. After all, we are human beings, just with varying degrees of social needs.

I spent the next few days debating which countries I would like to visit in Central and South America, but ultimately gave up as I wanted to stick to my preferred way of travel: Having no plan. Some of the most beautiful things had happened to me that way, and I wanted to remain open to all possibilities. I decided only on my starting point of Guatemala, Central America, and from there would work my way down to South

America. How exciting! I didn't speak any Spanish, to be honest, but why would that really matter? I had survived in all other regions of the world without speaking the local language. These days it is much easier with the help of digital translation and, additionally, the good old "hands and feet verbalization". My flight took off on the thirty-first of December. I celebrated New Year's on the plane and landed on the first of January in Guatemala City.

After I had explored the city for two days, I almost repeated my old pleasure-seeking, boilerplate patterns. I caught myself opening the dating apps and starting to swipe. Almost a routine process, a pattern so established that it happened basically unconsciously. You know, the same way you sometimes get to work but cannot remember the way because this routine is so deeply anchored in you that you can take your attention off it, think about other things, and still do it correctly. From here on, I decided that I had had enough. I was not willing to sacrifice costly travel time for meaningless pleasure any longer. From now on, I would only focus on dating if I saw the potential for something deeper to develop. I honestly wasn't interested in dull one-night stands anymore. I didn't need to experience more, different, or crazy things—I had had it (almost) all by now. My previous nervousness about potentially missing out on something sexual was no longer present. What I was actually missing out on was beyond the physical; it was love. Real love, in a form I had probably never experienced in the past. Pure and unconditional. Thankfully, I had finally reached my moment: I was done!

Two Years

The next day I took a taxi to Antigua, a beautiful, charming city with lots of old architecture and colorful buildings. I spent around a week there, simply enjoying walking around and exploring the neighborhood. One day, I was sitting in an Irish pub having a beer and talking to the bartender when a young woman in her late twenties came into the bar. We immediately caught each other's attention, looked the other in the eyes, and started a conversation. There was a strong attraction between us. I could not really grasp what exactly it was, but I wanted to talk to her to find out. A was from Guatemala. She told me her story, that she studied and worked, then quit and traveled in Europe for a while, and now was back in Antigua, where she lived with her friend (the bartender). I also told her my story and how I eventually ended up here in Antigua. We were fascinated by each other, feeling a good and positive energy between us. Something beyond the usual. Although our conversation lasted only for about fifteen minutes before she had to leave, I knew that I wanted to see her again. She told me that she worked as supervising manager in one of the nightclubs in Antigua and that I should come by next weekend. I said that I would leave for Lake Atitlan in two days but that I might come back afterward. And with that, our ways parted. It happened pretty quickly, and I did not have a chance to ask for her number. Maybe I indeed had to come back to see her again.

The next day, my last day in Antigua, I went to the same pub again to have a cold beer. Her friend, the barkeeper, was working again and indicated that A would also come later. Indeed, she did stop by, and I was happy to see her again. We continued our conversation from the previous night, this time exchanged numbers, and agreed that we would meet after I returned from the lake. Even though she was still young, she had a rather advanced view of the world and herself (her inner self). I understood that it was due to her going to therapy because of some things that had happened in her past. The old me would have avoided such cases at all costs, as it could realistically only bring trouble. However, the new me wasn't scared by that fact. It was more important for me to follow my intuition and find out more about her than to protect myself from potential complications that the situation might bring. And honestly, I was not the easiest candidate on this planet either—trouble was something I had caused more than enough of in the past. I was ready to look deeper than just the surface; superficial things such as appearance etc., were still part of the overall formula but no longer the main determining factor. I was mainly interested in the person and the unexplainable connection between us. Was that a sign that I had finally grown up? Was I mature enough by now to look for something more meaningful? Was she maybe the one? I didn't know, but what I definitely knew was that I would come back to find out. There was something worth exploring between us, and I would pin it down.

The following week at the lake was great—close to nature and with many small towns around to explore. A and I kept in touch during my absence, but unfortunately, we didn't get really deep in our conversations. While it was so easy and magical between us the first two times we met, I didn't feel the same depth or enthusiasm while we were texting. While interacting in person is something totally different, I also had pretty deep and exciting conversations via text in the past. Now it felt like the conversation was more forced than naturally flowing, something that would usually never be a good sign. Nevertheless, I reminded myself of the situation with C in Hanoi and that I had promised myself not to try to control those kinds of situations again in the future. I just accepted that we didn't get to know each other more during that week and looked forward to seeing her again in person instead. We agreed on a time to meet and were both excited to see each other soon.

She picked me up in her car as we were supposed to go somewhere for dinner. Instead, she parked in front of the same Irish pub where her friend, the bartender, worked; she just wanted to briefly say hi to her, apparently. I was a bit confused but followed along. It didn't really matter to me. After a while inside, she suggested having pizza and that her friend would join us as well. Now I was even more confused but didn't mind her friend joining us, as I genuinely liked her. So, the three of us went to the pizza place and talked about all sorts of things. Then A started asking me more personal questions that one would typically ask the other in a more private, date-type setting. I again didn't mind because I knew that the two were very close friends. A also made efforts for body contact, such as grabbing my hand or putting her hand on my shoulder or chest while talking to me. Quite honestly, the whole setup was rather odd. It was filled with mixed signals. Friend zone signals such as taking her best friend on our "date" without even telling me beforehand and dating signals with all the personal questions and targeted body contact. After a while, her friend had to go to work, and we sat together for a bit longer to talk until I walked her back to the car. Despite all the weirdness of that night, I liked A a lot. She had an interesting character, looked good, and had a very mature view on life that many women don't even have yet in their thirties. I definitely wanted to see her again.

The next day I texted her to check if and when we should meet for the coffee we'd agreed on the night before, but she suggested moving it due to period cramps. She indeed had her period coming the previous day, and hence I wasn't mad and simply spent the day by myself. We kept texting a little bit, but again there was no real flow. Why was it so difficult to talk to her via text but so easy in person? I wanted to know a lot of things about her and didn't have that much time left in Guatemala, but she didn't seem to feel the same urge.

I let her know that I wasn't ready to give this up yet and that I thought we should meet again to make sure we wouldn't regret anything in the future. While she agreed, all her text and voice messages had the tone of friendship, not the tone of dating, in them. Slowly, I started to realize that she simply had a different view on us, even though she clearly felt the same connection. However, she knew I was around for only a few more days and didn't want to risk any emotional drama. I wanted to see her nevertheless—there was nothing to lose. That night A worked at the nightclub and invited me to join. We chatted for a few minutes in the beginning, but then she obviously had to pursue her duties. She was basically running through the club all night, making sure everything was in order. I saw her sporadically, but we hadn't much time to talk.

In the end, I was pretty drunk and went straight home. She texted me a while later asking to join the afterparty, but I was already done with the night and had to sleep.

Again, another weird setup in which we met, and it didn't work well either. Nothing really seemed to flow easily. We both kind of wanted to see each other, but it always had a forced component to it. Then I just accepted that for her, it was more platonic, as she didn't see a practical future for us, while I was open to anything that would develop—such is life. Besides, A and her friend, the bartender, were pretty close; they lived together and spent the majority of their spare time with each other. I knew there was not really space for someone new like me who wouldn't fit into the existing setup. I had to accept it. Here I was again, same situation, different country. First C in Vietnam, now A in Guatemala. Both with a strong initial connection but no subsequent natural flow or follow-through. I also acknowledged my own mistakes; I partially wanted the other person to make me whole and happy instead of becoming both myself first. Any relationship would have a much better foundation on that basis, with less neediness and dependency on each other. How could it happen again in almost the same way? Did I need to learn more lessons? Was it all just preparation for something better to come? Did I have to let go even more? I wasn't sure. But I wouldn't give up! I knew it was possible to find true love on this journey. The intensity of those two initial connections with C and A were so encouraging that I had to dig further. Something special must be waiting for me out there.

I spent the last day deciding where I should go next. Still a bit sad from the events of the past week, but life had to go on. It made me stronger, after all. I decided to go to Costa Rica next, where I had the chance to be at the beach again, something I had been missing over the last few months. I drove back to Guatemala City, from where I would fly to San José the next day. Without me knowing or realizing it back then, that last night before my departure played a key role in the months to come. I checked in to the house close to the airport, bought some food, listened to some music, and basically just waited for the day to end. After dinner, I decided to play some soft alpha waves to relax.

The recording was unironically titled "Manifest Twin Flame Reunion". I had downloaded it a while ago but only listened to it for the first time that night. I lay down in bed in my typical meditation position, closed my eyes, and sank into the slow, rhythmic waves that brought a very deep sensation of peace and trust over me. I didn't aim to stop thinking or feeling but rather used my thoughts and emotions to support my visualization: I imagined letting A go, literally go, up into the air. I knew that if there would ever be a way for us, we would find each other again in the future. But for now, I had to let her go. I had to free myself from everything that had happened over the last weeks. All the pain, all the ups and downs that resulted from opening myself up to the possibility of finding real love. Maybe I was naïve. Maybe I was dreaming too much. But I deeply felt that I was close to something. That all these experiences were just preparation. That I had to keep going. That I had to go through the darkest valleys first to climb out on top of the brightest mountains later. Everything would turn out just perfect, as it always did. I had to let go, I had to trust, and I had to be ready to receive!

The meditation was very emotional; literally everything came out. Tears were rolling down my cheeks, a mix of surrender, sadness, and love. It felt good to let go; it took the ballast off my shoulders. I knew that I had to focus on myself for now, to forget about actively searching for something. It was time to get back to being whole without needing anything from the outside. I had been too focused on it over the last months, almost trying to force it. What I needed to do was take a step back. It was okay to want it, but I shouldn't *need* it. "Wanting but not needing" summarized my circumstances pretty well—if it happens, it happens; if not, then not. I would still be happy, love myself, and find my way. With or without finding someone else along the way to share experiences with. This moment was key for me as I opened the doors for my real soulmate or twin flame to enter my life. By letting go of everything (not needing) but simultaneously keeping the doors open for anything to happen (wanting), I sent out the exact matching frequency that would go into resonance with S from Colombia. I don't want to get into much more detail at this stage, but S did exactly the same thing on her end, in Colombia. We matched in the quantum field. From here on, everything was paved for us to eventually meet—none of the events of the following weeks were anything but destined to happen. Synchronicities were lining up one after another, until our paths finally crossed. Note that I did not know much about energy or frequency back then (i.e., constant radiation of frequency by way of electrical charge from our own thoughts and magnetic charge from our own emotions), but I realized a few months later what had happened during that night, and I am eternally grateful for it!

After the meditation, I was fully at peace and wanted to spend some more time on the topic of soulmate and twin flame. I had heard these terms before and roughly knew what to associate with them but had never dug deeper into it. Now was the perfect time, given I just had this profound experience by randomly listening to something titled this way. I spent the next hours reading articles and book excerpts, watching a number of educational videos, and then consolidating the key themes. On that basis, I summarized it as follows: We feel the other person to be (a part of) us, a reflection of ourselves, always connected no matter the distance. We want to form our relationship based on a shared purpose, growing together, instead of a fear-avoidance strategy aimed at making us whole. We strive for equal contributions, move away from selfishness to giving, and shed all our masks and fears. We will only meet our soulmate when both souls are ready; ready to transcend beyond our individual needs. We know that from this point onward, our lives will really begin—everything before is just preparation, to a certain extent.

I thought back to my past relationships and kind of knew that I had never really been in love. There was partnership, there was romance, and there were feelings, but I was never fully blown away. It never went further than a medium level of passion and excitement. I never wanted to make long-term plans with them. I was never ready to give more than to take. I was never willing to accept them unconditionally. Partially because I was emotionally not open enough in the past, but partially also because they were simply not the right ones. I knew that something more profound must be waiting to match with me at the exact right time in my life. Now was the time to be open, to be receptive to whatever would come. I was ready. Ready to grow and transcend together. My soulmate should be somewhere out there.

The next day I took off to Costa Rica. My destination was Jacó, at the beach that I had been missing for so long. It felt good to be by the ocean and the long beachfront. A sense of freedom with no buildings or mountains surrounding me for a change. Just the wide, uncapped view into the horizon with some of the most magnificent sunsets I had seen in a while—like a radiant ball of fire descending toward the horizon, reflecting onto the serene waters below, creating a seemingly endless fusion of light and color. I used those days to get back into shape by running every morning along the beach. Of course, I had also regularly hiked in the prior weeks, but the barefoot running on the beach in the quiet morning hours was something unique. It helped me to connect and ground myself. During the days, I would walk or bike around to explore the area, eat healthy food, and read a little. At night I didn't go out to bars at all—I simply wanted to spend time with myself.

Next, I booked a boat to Montezuma, a rather small and more "raw" destination with lots of nature around. It was again a beautiful place to continue my daily sports routine and to be at the beach. I didn't even swim that often, and I didn't have much interest in surfing either (when I studied abroad in

Australia during my B.Sc. I tried it a bit for fun but never really picked it up again). But I also didn't need to; all I wanted was to be close to the ocean, that was totally sufficient. I stayed for three days until I went back to Jacó, where I spent my thirty-fourth birthday at the end of January. No parties, no responsibilities, and no expectations—just the beautiful sunset at the beach. The sky was streaked with bright orange and pink as the sun set, the waves caressing the shore, and the wind gently blowing through my hair. One of the calmest birthdays I had ever had. I could not have wished for a better place to be. It was a short but great time in Costa Rica, with no distractions and pure focus on myself. The next morning, I took the bus back to the city, from where I flew to Bogotá, Colombia. It was the most sensible destination to start in South America, and from there, I would make my way across the continent.

I only spent one day in the city because I generally had enough of all the busyness. What was nice there in Colombia was that I could continue my preferred way of travel, in the sense of booking rooms in private houses somewhere in nature for a few days, then taking taxis to the next destination and staying another few days. At that point, I was already tired of taking frequent long flights. I wanted the destinations to be reachable by car and not too far from each other. I wasn't interested in seeing the main cities. I wanted to be in rural spots in nature without big crowds of people. In some countries, this way of travel wasn't easily possible, as there were not many possibilities to stay off-grid besides a few selected hotels, which I didn't really like to stay at in general. Consequently, I booked my first stop around two hours outside of Bogotá, at a beautiful family-owned cottage surrounded by the mountains. The family warmly welcomed me, and I immediately felt at home with them. Such a nice place, good vibe, and delicious home-cooked food. The first hours I explored the land, went for a run, and simply lay in the sun to read and journal a bit.

I thought about the last months and decided to write C from Vietnam a final text to come clean with the situation; I apologized for how I had behaved and expressed my certainty that she would find her perfect match soon. It wasn't the time to point fingers anymore, or to let my hurt ego dictate the way I behaved. It was time to simply be nice and leave the situation behind. Funnily enough, she replied to my text and asked to talk on the phone. It was much easier now, with no strings or expectations attached, just a platonic conversation between two "old friends". She updated me on her situation, how she was occasionally still looking around a bit but with less focus on the whole dating thing overall. I agreed with her that this was the right approach and that I was basically doing the same. We wished each other all the best for the future and thereby closed our short chapter together peacefully. Coincidentally, the next day was A's (from Guatemala) birthday, which I had saved in my calendar during our first date. I decided that I should also text her to wish her a happy birthday, without expecting anything from it. I simply wanted to be friendly and congratulate her in good manners. It would probably also help me to close the situation with her in peace. I texted her, and that was it. I came clean, with C and with A, and that way finally got over my hurt ego. After all, none of what had happened was anybody's fault; it simply wasn't meant to be.

On that day, I also decided to give the dating apps another try. I hadn't checked them for several weeks and honestly didn't feel the need to. I was happy to focus on myself and to fully enjoy nature, first in Costa Rica and now in Colombia. I didn't need anyone else to make me feel good or whole. I was it already myself. Exactly that ease was what I had lost before— now I could approach the whole situation with indifference. If a promising opportunity would pop up, great, but if not, then it wouldn't matter either. My natural flow was back, and it felt great. No pressure, no expectations, no neediness. Simply openness to all possibilities. I swiped a bit left and right without any deeper intentions or desires attached to it, and a few minutes later, let it be. I didn't want to waste this beautiful day on my phone, as it was my only day at the cottage. The next morning I took off for my next destination.

An English woman married to a Colombian man, and their two kids, lived on the land further up the mountains. Over the years, they had built a few traditional mud houses, of which they rented out two to guests. My tiny house was directly on the mountaintop with a view down the whole valley. A hammock hung on the porch, and I could simply lie down, watch, take in the scenery, and be fully present in those beautiful moments. From time to time, their two dogs would come by to visit me and find a comfortable place in the shade below my hammock or under the table. What a wonderful combination of everything; pure nature, lovely animals, and total silence. Each night we shared dinner, exchanged stories, and laughed a lot together. It was perfect. I don't know what exactly it was that made the Colombian people in those rural territories so happy, whole, and satisfied. None of the country's geopolitical problems could be felt there; everything had a positive baseline to it.

The first night, I decided to open the dating app again to see if something interesting had popped up from my swipes the day earlier. A few things here and there, as usual, but nothing I wanted to explore in more depth. However, one match caught my interest, nevertheless. Naturally, with those apps, you are forced to judge your counterpart mainly by their appearance. I looked at her pictures and honestly wasn't that excited at first, but there was something unique about her, especially her eyes. It was something outside the typical criteria I would usually look for, yet very prepossessing.

Her first text introduction to me was very original, a classy "Hey"—what else could you expect from those apps, right? Everybody has their own tactic, if you want to call it that, at least from the guys' side. Girls, on average, have a bit of a simpler game. A one-word line was often sufficient for them to succeed. Anyway, I replied with a likewise classy "Hey S, I like your style!" for which she thanked me and asked how I was. "Very good. I am currently in nature outside the city and love it. And you?" I responded. From there, our conversation continued, and shortly after, we agreed to potentially meet in Bogotá when I returned from my nature trips in a little over a week. Do you remember when I said the conversations with A always felt somewhat forced and not naturally flowing? It was totally different between S and me. We could talk for hours about all sorts of topics. I would show her the area where I was, she would tell me about her work in the hospital (medical student), and so on. I would ask a few personal questions, and she would add on from her side thereafter. It was a harmonic interplay of giving and taking, of listening and talking, precisely how any good conversation should be.

At that point, we were probably both thinking that this would be a one-time thing; I only had one available day upon my return to the city before I took off to Ecuador (the Galapagos Islands). I was honest with her about it, but we agreed to meet regardless. While she would have preferred at least a few days to enjoy each other's company until the initial bliss was over (as it typically was in those short-term interactions), she also felt this connection between us was worth exploring and therefore was likewise as keen to meet me as I was to meet her, even if it would be for one time only. Over the next week, our conversations became really deep. Something that usually never happens on those apps. If a potential date is too far out, people either lose interest, find someone else in the meantime, or simply stop talking. It was completely different for us. We would text almost throughout the whole day. Initially, not all the time, but at least every few hours. And later more frequently. Neither of us had to think about the way, intervals, or content we wrote; it just happened naturally, and we both felt it. Neither of us was playing games, trying to artificially make ourselves interesting. It was real and honest. Exactly what I was hoping for.

What I especially liked was our similarity in terms of worldview. She wasn't religious either and had spent some time on the topics around spirituality herself. She knew there are so many things we—as humans—simply don't know yet about our existence. The universe beyond the observable galaxies remains largely unexplored. Nobody can say with certainty how many universes there may potentially be, or if they are even infinite. With that in mind, is there maybe more to life than how we perceive it here on Earth? We exchanged theories, expanded our views, and learned new perspectives from each other. It felt good to openly talk with someone about it, without needing to worry about the other being judgmental or feeling ashamed. I had finally found someone who understood. S and I were on the same wavelength.

My next stop was in Suesca, an area famous for rock climbing. Here I stayed in a cabin directly in front of the gigantic rock: A tranquil ambiance with unparalleled panoramic views. The rustling of leaves in the breeze, the distant calls of birds soaring through the sky, and the babbling of the nearby stream gently enriched the overall experience acoustically. It was perfect. The owner kindly let me borrow his bike so that I could make my daily tour to the town to buy groceries. This simple way of life I had learned to love most during the last year. Being in nature, going on long walks to explore the area, buying fresh groceries to cook, and most importantly, no distractions in the form of restaurants, bars, or clubs. Such beauty in this simplicity. Nothing else was needed. I felt much happier by myself in these surroundings than within a big crowd in the big cities. I practically became part of whichever area I stayed in and was fully satisfied just being in the moment, not at all on the lookout for the next exciting thing to eat, drink, or do. I was at peace with myself, able to endure my thoughts and shadows, and comfortable giving up control. I noticed my own behavior gradually changing for the better and was a bit proud of myself, too. I still had a long way to go, but at least I was walking in the right direction.

S told me that she had a somewhat turbulent time at home and moved out rather early. She went to therapy (as did A from Guatemala), which helped her better understand herself, the human experience, and the world in general. Again, I wasn't scared by that fact because the person behind it was what fascinated me. To the contrary, I found that both S and A were much more mature than many other, much older people—the therapies accelerated their internal growth process. S and I hadn't even met each other in person yet became so close by texting alone. From my experiences with C and A, I knew that I would need to simply let this situation unfold naturally. I would not expect, force, or need anything from her. I would just enjoy our conversations and be grateful for exactly that. Anything else on top of it would be purely optional.

Over time, we realized that we had so many similarities that it was almost a bit scary. Literally everything seemed to match, from small daily things to bigger topics of life, from preferences, habits, and hobbies to views on family, spirituality, and death. S was practically a younger, female version of myself. To that point, I had barely seen or heard of something similar in other couples and had definitely not experienced it in my past relationships. For illustration purposes, let us take an example of the overall percentage match with a respective partner: I am sure most of us would say there is no 100 percent match. It usually is somewhere between 70 to 80 percent, to pick a number. S and me, on the other hand, seemed to be at or above 90 percent. I was blown away by those similarities and was more than ready to explore them further. It was something special. Intriguing. In that context, I also thought about my past relationships and concluded that my ex-girlfriends usually represented the opposite of me; a calmer part, the balancing "good girl". However, what was often missing was the passion, the fire in the relationship. Maybe that passion and fire would not come from opposing characteristics to mine, but rather the same to mine. Maybe the more than 90 percent overlap with S could be exactly that.

Next, I went to a small farm with a few horses, goats, dogs, and pigs. It was a wonderful place in nature where I enjoyed every single minute with the animals. That was another key takeaway from my travels—I really loved being around animals. While I saw them as just that, animals, in the past, I had started to really feel a deeper connection to them over the last year. I saw them as my friends. Companions for an unspecified period of time. Whenever and wherever I would encounter them. Maybe it was just for a few minutes when I petted a dog on the street, or a few hours when I visited certain places where they were home, or even a few days when I stayed at places like this farm. It was easy to bond with them; they didn't demand anything besides a little attention or food. Over time, it became easier for me to understand them, to relate to them. Once we put aside the perspective of ourselves versus the outer world, we are able to feel the connection with animals as well. After all, they share the same cosmic source as all of us humans do, pure consciousness. Now, are really all animal species self-aware? We don't know. But do we know with certainty that all of us humans are? No, though we should at least all have the capability.

One night S didn't feel well. She ate a few "sleeping gummy bears" (to help one to fall asleep) too many and felt dizzy. She texted me saying that she thought she had screwed up, to which I answered suggesting not to panic. I offered to talk on the phone, and she immediately called. I calmed her down, simply being there for her, providing the comfort of not being alone in that situation. She couldn't talk much as she felt the dizziness increase; hence I decided to tell her a few fun stories about my past. I felt that she needed me at this moment, and I wanted to be there for her. I knew it couldn't have been anything really serious as these were rather light substances, nothing requiring a prescription. We talked for over an hour, and she had become much calmer at the end. Tiredness had replaced the initial panic.

This simple act of selflessness, kindness, and compassion would have been rather unusual for the old me. More likely, I would have told her not to overreact, try to sleep, and then leave her on her own. I would have simply applied the situation to myself and imagined how I would have reacted, and then assumed that she could or should react in the same way. Things that weren't a big deal for me should also not be a big deal for others, I would have assumed. I was both happy and surprised to see myself act completely differently here—not because I had to or thought it would be the right thing to do, but wanting to do it from my heart. One of the meaningful moments that showed me what it means to live from the heart rather than the mind. The next morning, S texted to thank me and couldn't remember much of the conversation. I assured her she didn't spill any crazy secrets, and we laughed together. Even though it was not that huge of an event in itself (everything is relative in the end), it was an important situation for us to become closer. She knew she could count on me; I knew I had helped her gladly.

My last stop was where I had initially started, at the family-owned cottage. The place was so nice and welcoming that I had to come back. I spent another two days there before I made my way back to Bogotá, where S and I would finally meet. Back in the city, I checked in to my hotel, took a shower, had a beer while waiting for her, and finally jumped into her taxi on the way to the bar we wanted to go to. We sat down, ordered a drink, and started talking. She looked so much better in person than in the pictures. Her eyes were uniquely shaped, somewhat mixed between Latin and Asian, big and pitch black. Her skin was so perfect, so soft. She didn't wear any makeup at all. She was a natural beauty. I loved it. More importantly, we could also talk smoothly in person. We recapped the events of the previous week, my travel, her work, and our respective histories. It was a wonderful time we spent together, and we were both relieved that our "random" match had turned out that well. Even though she had a practical exam at the hospital the next morning, she still wanted to meet me. I clearly noticed the differences between C, A, and S—she made an effort to see me regardless of feeling stressed by the upcoming exam. She was ready to take a step in my direction and was actually interested in meeting me. While C and A had simply canceled when they didn't feel well or planned to do other things, S took the initiative and made it happen nevertheless. It was an equal contribution from both of us. We both wanted it. We both knew it.

Two drinks later, we decided to go to my hotel; despite our long and deep conversations over the last week, we both still assumed this would likely be a one-time thing. Our hours in the hotel were unforgettably intimate and passionate, deeply bonding us in person. A fearless and shameless interplay of our deepest desires. We allowed it all to happen. We set ourselves free. During our act, I also noticed the different scars around her body. She had quite a few of them, same as me. While I would have probably judged and disliked such superficial things in any other woman, with S, I didn't care at all. Rather to the contrary, I loved those scars on her. They made her unique. They made her interesting. They made her stand out from the rest. I wanted her exactly that way and not a single bit different. For me, she was perfect. Her appearance, her body, her voice, her character, her being.

S told me that she usually would not kiss or cuddle much unless she felt really connected to the other person. It was the same for me; not even with my ex-girlfriends was I that deep into those things. Of course, we hugged and kissed each other, but it was rather short-lived and usually not that intense. With S, it was different—after multiple rounds, we were still hugging, kissing, and caressing each other for another two hours. Not much talking at all. Simply lying in bed together, letting this strong bond happen. I could feel her breath, her sweat, and her heat on my body. I heard her heart beating. And I pressed her closer to me. Simultaneously, I sensed something happening on the non-physical level. There was an intense flow of energy between the two of us, highly conscious, full of joy, bliss, and love. No thinking, and no evaluating, just total presence. Lying in stillness. It was as if our souls had merged during that time. We practically became one outside of our physical bodies. Something I had never experienced before.

After the last meaningless one-night stands in Nepal, where I didn't even feel the usual cheap dopamine kick any longer, now I was lucky enough to experience the complete opposite. Two people, who would typically protect their own feelings and block all unnecessary emotions, acting together in a completely different way: Allowing that beautiful symbiosis to happen, unifying on a level beyond matter, becoming one! After a while, I accompanied S down to her taxi as she had to sleep at least a few hours before her exam the next day. We thanked each other for that wonderful night, not knowing if we would ever meet again. But that didn't matter—what mattered was this unforgettable night had happened. It was something unique to remember, to never forget.

When I woke up the next morning, I knew exactly what I had to do—push back my flight to Ecuador. I had initially planned to stay in Quito for two days before flying to the Galapagos Islands. But I honestly didn't need those two days and therefore decided to prolong my stay in Bogotá. S and I met again the following day, had dinner, and went to my hotel. It was another great night together, nothing short of the wonderful first one. As I had to check out of my hotel the next day, S offered to let me stay at her place until my departure. It was not only sexual attraction between us but also the simple act of being together. Things felt so easy, good, and natural with her, as if we had known each other for years already. We walked around the city, played arcade games in the shopping mall, had delicious breakfasts, and lay for hours in bed together. It was a perfect combination of everything. To that point, we both didn't think much about what would happen once I left. We just allowed ourselves to enjoy the experience to the fullest without rationally questioning it. On my day of departure, we agreed to see and feel how our relationship would develop from here; due to my travels, we couldn't plan anything specific. Maybe it was just a short-term holiday romance, but maybe it could also become something more. We were fully aligned to not control or force anything but to take it step by step along the way to a potential reunion in the future. We were not sad that it was over; we were grateful that it happened.

I arrived at the airport and was ready to check in my luggage for the flight to Ecuador. As with many South American countries, one needs to show proof of a return or onward flight before being allowed to board the plane. However, I hadn't booked such a flight in advance. In fact, I hadn't thought about my next destination at all, and consequently had to decide within ten minutes where I would go next. I checked the map, scrolled up and down, zoomed in and out, but it wasn't really conclusive. First, I thought about Peru but remembered there was political unrest in the country and that many tourist attractions, including Machu Picchu, had been shut down just days before. Next, I thought about Brazil but didn't know much about the country besides the two big cities, Rio de Janeiro and

São Paulo. Then I thought about the last three magical days with S—our unique connection to each other. Why not come back to Colombia afterward to see her again? After all, I was free. Nothing stood against us seeing each other besides my own fears and rational thinking patterns. What we had shared was special, something that I would not be willing to simply let go of unless we both decided to. Almost instantly, I booked my return ticket to Bogotá, not giving my ego-self the slightest chance to destroy any of this with rationality or logic. I figured that around ten days would be enough time for me to sufficiently explore the islands, and thereafter I would come back to see S again. I checked in my luggage, went through security procedures, and updated her on the latest developments. She was as happy as I was that we would indeed see each other again, and so soon.

The Galapagos Islands were really impressive. A living testament to the beauty of nature and wildlife. They provide home to a diversity of animals, such as giant tortoises, blue-footed boobies, sea lions, and marine iguanas. The lovely part is that one can get very close to these animals. For example, I regularly tanned in the sun surrounded by seals and iguanas, almost like a group of friends hanging out at the beach. They even tried to appropriate my towel a few times but without success. Though I definitely lost the "fight" for the bench in the shade, on which they preferred to relax during the hot afternoon sun. Of course, I had to respect their territory, otherwise they would become rather aggressive. They didn't like anybody coming too close or even dare sitting on their bench. It was theirs! Such fun times with these guys.

Max Tower

I spent the first few days on Santa Cruz Island, where most of the happenings take place. While there were quite a few tourists, the island still had a traditional flair to it. I rented a bike to explore each corner of the island, ate the most delicious seafood, and met a few very nice people in my hostel. One of them was a young woman from France around my age. She had a similar story to mine, and we talked about our individual paths. I also told her about what had just happened to me in Colombia, and she looked at me and said, "I wish the same would happen to me!" Do you know the funny part about it? I had used those exact same words just a few weeks before in Guatemala; I spoke to someone at the Irish pub who told me her story about how she met a guy from Europe on his travels who later became her boyfriend. "I wish the same would happen to me!" was exactly what I had said to her back then—and it indeed happened. It is so interesting how circumstances are sometimes so interconnected with each other, forming synchronicities all along the way. The French woman and I became friends pretty quickly; we visited the giant tortoise farm together and cycled down from the Highlands back to the port of the island. She was a very nice person, and I sincerely hoped she would have a chance to experience the same thing along the way.

My next stop was Isabella Island, which I really liked. It was so raw, so underdeveloped, and so much calmer. Mostly locals lived on the island, as the few tourists mainly came for day tours via boat. The island had magnificent beaches; I could pick up my early morning running routine again. The sun would slowly rise and reflect on the shimmery surface of the wet sand. No one else was around in these early morning hours. Just me, jogging barefoot along the beach, and a few hungry birds trying to catch their breakfast in the sand or sea. It was beautiful. Impressions that I will never forget. S and I kept texting and talking during all that time—she basically participated from a distance, although it almost felt as if she were with me. There was no pressure behind it, no expectations. We simply let things happen and swam with the natural flow. Isn't it fascinating how we can feel so close to someone that is geographically so far away, yet feel so distant to others who are in proximity to us? Apparently, there must be something else connecting us beyond the physical realm. I would find out precisely that in the not-so-distant future.

I decided to go back to Santa Cruz for the last three days, as I didn't want to travel for hours on the boat between the remaining islands. I was completely happy and satisfied with the impressions I got and just wanted to relax for the remaining time. I made myself fresh salads or sandwiches for lunch and would eat out for dinner. On my last night, I drove around the island to find a quiet place to eat. It was very busy outside as there was some kind of local carnival event happening. Most restaurants were packed with people. I noticed a side street with a small restaurant and a few empty chairs in front. Nobody was eating there. It was a small pizzeria owned by a local man. I checked online for reviews, but he didn't even have any presence there yet. I talked to him to understand how the business was going and felt the insecurity and sadness in his voice. His business was not going too well in general. People were eating along the busy main road, but nobody came to his place, it seemed. I decided that I should at least be his customer for the night and ordered a veggie pizza to go. He didn't have any cartons for takeaway either. "Oof, so what do we do now?" I asked him.

"I don't know. I'm sorry," he said.

"Let me drive down the road and get a carton from the other pizza place. But your pizza better be good!" I responded with a smile and swung on my bike to get the carton. In the end, I decided to eat half the pizza at his restaurant anyway, as he was so nice and had no customers that night. At least the two of us could spend a bit of time together.

While I was eating at the table outside, he was also positioned with his advertisement board in front of the restaurant, trying to win potential new guests, but nobody would bite. "Pizza, pizza. Delicious pizza!" he shouted around without success, as most people simply went on to the main street. It was so sad to see; a man with his dreams of independence mainly crushed by a disadvantageous location. Yes, situations like those are common everywhere, but here I could really feel and share his desperation and sadness. The pizza itself was really good, so I decided to give him a tip worth a few multiples of the actual price. It didn't hurt me to give that money away, and it helped him a lot to turn this otherwise sad day around. It felt good to share with him not only the money but, more importantly, the time and companionship. We fixed a few typos on his advertisement board together and enjoyed a digestive cup of tea. It was a lovely, spontaneous encounter between us. Frankly, these are the moments that make life special, regardless of where we are in this world. These tiny moments of love and compassion are what make our human experience so beautiful and unique. I know, these days we are all stressed, need to look out for ourselves first, and make sure our familes are properly taken care of. But sharing a bit of time and attention is something we all could do. Over the last year, I had felt increasingly more joy in giving than taking, and that was a wonderful thing to witness.

The next day I flew back to Colombia to meet S again. We booked a small cabin one hour outside the city to spend the weekend together in nature. We went on walks, cooked our own meals, and explored the small neighboring town. It felt as if we had been in a relationship for years already. We worked seamlessly as a team and had almost no conflicts. I was well aware that this vacation-like time together was nothing comparable to an actual relationship with the ups and downs of daily life, but at least it was a good indicator that the two of us were highly compatible. If a conflict popped up, we both stepped forward to solve it swiftly. Neither of us remained in their ego-position of "I am right"; that was an important sign for me. I am sure most of us will know from experience that with some people, this simple act of forgiving and moving on is rather simple, while with others, it can become a nightmare. Thus, I was grateful that we not only shared so many commonalities in life but also in solving our disagreements. After the weekend, we spent another two days in the city together before it was time for me to move on again. We discussed that we should keep our approach the same as we had done until now: Don't force, simply flow. It had worked so well until now, and we didn't want to destroy it with attachments to illusory long-term plans (or rather dreams). In early March, I landed in Rio de Janeiro, Brazil.

Rio was extremely hot and busy. I stayed in an apartment at the Copacabana, where I would go on runs in the mornings and then mostly cycle around with my borrowed bike. The atmosphere in the center was pretty dense—it was hot, lots of pickpockets, and generally too many people crammed in too little space. However, along the beach road, it was better, and that was where I spent most of my time. Watching the talented footvolley players doing their tricks, enjoying a few fresh coconuts, and simply merging with the crowds along the long beachfront. I was eating pretty clean and also hadn't drunk any alcohol since I had left Guatemala. I didn't feel the need at all and enjoyed staying sober much more, savoring the day rather than the night. I also noticed my general mood had lightened up over the last weeks. Partly based on my changed eating and drinking patterns, but partly also based on my interactions with S. We kept talking daily, and it was great to have her practically with me. She was the perfect travel companion from a distance.

After a few days, I noticed the frequency and manner of texting had changed. She wasn't so talkative any longer, and I could sense that something was off. I called her to check if everything was okay, but she sounded very confused and didn't want to talk much. Later she texted me explaining that she felt like she was losing control, that some unknown feeling had emerged inside her, but she couldn't pin down what exactly it was. We discussed that maybe she needed some more time for herself, besides her work in the hospital, and whether she should try to do more sports or meet more people after work, for example. "Phases like these come and go. I had a few of them myself in the past. And they always went away after a while," was all the advice that I could offer at that point. I spent the next day thinking whether she maybe had more hidden issues than she initially told me, but I didn't want my fears and judgments to ruin that wonderful experience between us. I had to make sure my ego-self would not get in control and push her away. I had to be with her during that situation. After all, that was what I had planned to do more frequently in the future—to help other people, and to give more than to take. She asked me to stick with her during this "weird" time of hers, and I confirmed that I would be there for her. The next day, she told me that her mom would come to visit her for a few days. I felt a sense of relief knowing that she wouldn't be alone. The two of them went camping outside the city for a few days to simply enjoy some mom-and-daughter time together. It helped S a lot. Sometimes all we need is to be with family, feeling secure and protected. Even though I had been independent for years, I regularly enjoyed and valued my time with family at home in between my travel destinations. It felt good to know there was always a safe space to return to.

In the meantime, I had moved to the next destination, two driving hours away from the buzzing Copacabana. I rented an apartment in a rather small town with no tourism and spent the rest of my time there. It was directly on the beachfront so that I could hear the waves when going to bed at night and when waking up in the mornings. The perfect location to continue my sports routine and advance my cooking skills. I didn't feel the need to explore the whole country; I was happy around the area of Rio. After almost two years, I was definitely a bit tired of moving around every few days, and for now, I just wanted to stay in one place a bit longer. During those days, I also started listening to pure isochronic and binaural gamma waves for at least half an hour each day. There are quite a few studies confirming the benefits of regular intake of 40 hz gamma frequencies, such as improved mood, cognitive functions, and memory.[6-8] During my travels, I certainly hadn't used as much brain power as I'd used to in the past and hence decided that I should at least try it out. The monotonous frequency had a very calming effect on me, the perfect supplement for my daily walks along the beach. I reached a state of very high consciousness on many of the walks, also thanks to those gamma waves. I decided to keep the experiment running for at least a month—certainly an important preparation factor for what would happen a few weeks later in Switzerland. It was mid-March by now, S felt much better, and I decided that I would visit her one last time before flying home at the end of March. One of my best friends had his bachelor party on the last weekend of the month, and I had to be back by then; I was his best man and organized our upcoming tour while on the road.

S and I spent another wonderful four days together in the same manner as we did before. Nothing had changed. If anything, we were even closer by now, despite the regular interruptions from my travels. Our day to say goodbye had come, and we reflected on this inimitable experience we were so lucky to share with each other. We seemed to have a complementing balance of traditionally considered masculine and feminine traits within each one of us that, together, would form this beautiful, harmonic interplay of our souls and minds. I had evolved my feminine side over the last two years of travel (e.g., more emotional, less rational) while she had grown her masculine side (e.g., independence, goal-oriented) from the day she lived alone. It was the perfect combination of both traits in her and me that balanced us so seamlessly. Likely, we wouldn't want to have two people dominated by the same traits in our relationship. Such setups could maybe work for a transitional period of change but ultimately would need balancing again, in my view.

All the small things, e.g., her having exactly those days off when I would come to visit her, or finishing one of her exams exactly one day before I would come to see her, worked in our favor. There was no forcing at all; circumstances simply aligned for us. Both of us wanted the same thing, to the same degree. And we received it. We realized: That is how it feels when something is destined to happen—the universe (or any other force, whatever you may call it) will make sure everything is aligned for you to create that experience. It was indeed magical. When I compared the flow of events with C or A in the months before, I definitely knew that those two were only preparation for me to eventually meet S, my actual destination. Honestly, I fell a bit in love with her during those few days we shared in Colombia. The tight bond between us, the connection without words when we looked deep into each other's eyes, when we really saw each other. Of course, we were also scared to fully give in to those feelings, but we were ready to take the risk. We didn't know if and when we would ever meet again, and we didn't know if and how we would continue communicating after I left, but we knew that we were ready to find out. As before, we agreed to take it step by step and see how our relationship would develop—in our specific scenario, there was no planning possible. I had no idea where I would be in a few months while she had to continue her studies in Bogotá. All we had were our marvelous memories together that neither of us would ever forget. I knew that I had found my soulmate.

My return flight to Germany was from Guatemala (where I had started my trip), and hence I spent the last three days in Antigua. In the taxi from Guatemala City to Antigua, I looked out the window, simply letting the memories of those last two years pass by. I was in a total state of peace. Everything was perfect as it was. I didn't want to change a single thing that had happened during my travels, good or bad. I realized that without all the painful experiences during my quest for money, quest for purpose, and quest for love, I would not be where I was right now. All events had been connected to each other. Everything had to happen the way it happened. Whoever I encountered on the way was exactly who I had to meet. It was a beautiful and vivid picture forming right in front of my eyes. Then, completely spontaneously, never having had a single thought about it before, it came to me: I need to write a book about it. A book titled *Two Years*. All these experiences, all these emotions, all these losses, all these gains, all these ups, all these downs. It was almost enough material to make a movie. However, what I should do instead is write a book. I

Two Years

had read so many different books during my travels; some were personal stories, and some were factual. But none of them really combined the two. That is where I saw my niche: A combination of personal story and educational material using my own real-life examples. I always preferred to guard my private life and certainly wasn't keen to disclose all those negative events and characteristics about me—but that is exactly what a reader of a good book would actually want, right? To be on the journey alongside the protagonist, to see what he sees, to feel what he feels, to grow with him. In my state of bliss and high consciousness, I wrote down the table of contents (exactly as it is in the book!) with key bullet points within less than an hour. I was in a state of total flow, as if a higher guidance was at work, leading my fingers while typing. Everything that had happened over the last two years suddenly came together in one beautiful piece. What a feeling!

The Grand Finale

After two days at home, I had to leave again for my friend's bachelor party weekend. It was great to have our old group reunited and enjoy the time together; the weekend was a perfect mix of fun, games, and nightlife, and all of us were very happy. Afterward, I spent another week at home, as my mom wanted to go on a short vacation—something she hadn't done in a while—and I made sure my grandma, who is in her late eighties and lives in the house next door, would be all right during that time.

I was still in this wonderful mode of love, peace, and joy from my South America trip and decided to dig further into the depths of brain waves. The one-month gamma waves experiment was going very well and definitely contributed to my sustained heightened awareness, as well as overall mood enhancement. I realized that over the previous years, while under constant pressure from work, my brain had been mostly operating under beta waves, typical for the state of alertness and focus, but also stress. In beta, we tend to act from competition rather than oneness, a feeling of separation—you versus me, often related to the evolutionary fight-or-flight mode. It was also possible for me to get into a flow state during those times, but certainly nothing comparable to the high consciousness states (as if guided by a higher power) in gamma, which not only makes extreme focus possible but, at the same time, also provides an overarching feeling of insight and connectedness—to source, to others, to everything.

Our brains consist of billions of neurons that predominantly communicate via electrical charges. When groups of those neurons fire together to send signals to other groups of neurons, the resulting patterns are commonly referred to as brainwaves, which can be of lower or higher frequency, ranging from delta to gamma. By listening to specific waves/frequencies, we support our brain getting into the desired state via brainwave synchronization, i.e., the brainwaves will naturally synchronize to the rhythm of external stimuli such as music. On that basis, I established a routine for my walks during the day and meditations at night. During my walks, I would predominantly listen to gamma or alpha frequencies; alpha helps to relax the body and mind, with both literally wandering freely in those moments. My brain and heart would thereby become highly coherent, and those walks had a somewhat therapeutic effect in the form of walking meditation (slow, rhythmic, and monotonous). At night, during my end-of-day meditations, I would mainly listen to theta waves. In that state between wakefulness and sleep, our subconscious becomes most receptive to new information, i.e., we can best reprogram our mind, patterns, and beliefs (delta waves are mainly associated with deep sleep and were thus less relevant for my purposes). Beta waves I avoided altogether, as I had had enough of them, not only over the years at work but also during my general days when I wasn't specifically aware of my inner state of being. While I won't go into further detail here, the interested reader may choose to independently dive deeper into the topic of brainwaves.[9,10]

However, I also understood that if I wanted to sustainably change my way of life and my attitude toward it, I had to adjust my own base frequency throughout the whole day, not only while meditating or walking in nature. I had to remind myself daily not to give in to doubts and fears of the unknown future now that I was back in my home country, "back to reality", so to speak. While it was easy to remain in those higher frequencies when I was physically farther away, it naturally got a bit harder back in my known environment, where almost everybody acts, thinks, and feels the same way. Therefore, I had to define new structures and tools that would support my envisaged way forward. I couldn't just go back to "normal" from here; I had to understand what else was possible my way.

I didn't tell anyone about my book idea either. Generally, I never shared much with other people until it was permanent. The expectations, opinions, and grudges of other people would mostly have net negative impacts on such plans, at least in my experience. I preferred to keep it private and only share the end results when I wanted to. In addition, I hadn't even progressed beyond the initial idea, and there were still a lot of open questions and doubts. For example, I was still doubting whether the material would be interesting enough to write about, if I would be a talented enough writer, if I could even fill a whole book with the events and experiences, and if I wanted to disclose all that private information about me after all. I figured that the book should ideally have an additional component to it, something that makes it stand out among all the others, that makes it unique. But what could that be? Was there any special content I should include? Did I experience anything that no one had ever experienced before? That wasn't particularly the case. Yes, my story was good, but nothing that the world had never seen or heard before. It needed to be something else. Somehow, it should also put the reader, practically speaking, the customer, in the center. Like any good consumer product does. I couldn't figure it out quite yet, but I came closer.

Of course, I also spent time thinking about what I wanted, should, or could do in the long run with my life. I thought back to the days of me being in the office, working in diverse teams, across divisions, always driven by the next deal. It wasn't that bad, after all; I had enjoyed it for a long time. But my passion for it had vanished. I couldn't force it to come back and probably wouldn't be happy by just starting again exactly where I had left almost two years ago. I didn't know what to do yet, and I also felt that I wasn't ready to pin anything concrete down. There was an inner feeling that told me to wait a bit more and that everything would become clear soon. At the same time, I also knew that my exotic world travel was over at that point—I had seen and experienced everything I wanted to see and experience, it was the perfect amount of travel. If I had simply continued to explore the rest of the world, I would have been one of those people who just keep going based on lack of alternatives. There is generally nothing wrong with that. Everybody can do whatever they want. But I didn't want that for myself. I didn't want to travel for longer. I felt that I was done for the time being and that now the next stage of my life was about to begin. I was just a bit unclear on what exactly it would look like.

I decided that I would finish my two years of travel in Switzerland, a country of beautiful nature, many mountains, and friendly people. It was very comparable to Austria in these aspects, and after all, I had spent such wonderful and transformational weeks there in March the year before. It was the perfect place to end my trip and explore options to potentially move to Switzerland long-term—I was open to anything. An exciting finale lay right ahead of me. The second week of April, my mom returned from her vacation, I packed my suitcase, and subsequently boarded the train to Lucerne, my first stop.

I immediately felt at home there. After all the different cultures and impressions over the last months, I enjoyed being in Europe again. While I was seeking the contrast before, now I wanted to be around people similar to me. I mean, in the end, we are all similar, all made out of the same tiny things—atoms. Which in turn are made of electrons, protons, and neutrons. And the latter two, on an even deeper level, are made of (assumed indivisible) particles called quarks—a fast-moving point of energy. So, in the end, we are all made of energy and thereby are technically the same. However, we usually do not perceive ourselves as such, as we aren't taught to. We are raised to see ourselves as matter, the human body that is separate from others. We believe that different cultures and environments shape us at the core, whereas these are actually just outside factors shaping our (partially acquired) personality.

I noticed the desire to read books coming up inside me again, something I hadn't done much in the last half year. Similar to how I did it in Austria, I spent a few hours each day in bookstores and libraries, where I found exactly what I needed and wanted to read. This time, I focused less on topics such as soul versus mind, as I had already done my work on that front last year, but more on the topics of energy and frequency. Over the last years, we as a society have partially progressed from seeing these topics as spirituality to actual science (e.g., quantum physics). I was fascinated by the theme and wanted to really understand what was behind it. While I had read a few high-level introductions and listened to a few podcasts on those topics before, it never fully clicked in the sense of it becoming an actual belief of mine. For that, I needed to dig deeper. Needed to connect the dots of the individual bits and pieces I found in the different sources. My four-week journey began.

Besides the reading, I also continued my exploration walks around the city, mostly with my earphones in, continuing my gamma waves experiment. During and after those walks, I had some of my most conscious and highly energetic moments of the last few years. It is a state of being difficult to describe, but the whole body feels electrically charged with ample energy that needs to be channeled or "unloaded" somewhere and somehow. In addition, one is in a state of heightened awareness during those times—for example, tones and colors are much more intense, and vision, in general, becomes extremely sharp. While we usually walk around not noticing the majority of things or happenings around us, focusing on only one specific thing (e.g., a conversation, a tree, or a dog), during those highly conscious moments, seemingly everything becomes the center of attention, the focus, at once. A state of enhanced cognitive functioning that can be a little scary at first (remember, the ego wants to control, to remain in its known state of being) but all the more exciting once accustomed to it. We begin to understand that we are capable of so much more but simply don't know how to unlock those powers yet. Meditation, either by sitting or lying still or by walking, is one tool supporting us to achieve exactly that.

I began to wonder what precisely the use of those heightened awareness states was. Don't get me wrong, I liked them as they were, and it was a great feeling in itself to walk around in sharpness and connectedness with everything. But shouldn't there also be more practical uses for it? We still cannot predict the future or guess the winning lottery numbers with it (at least, I think not), but we can certainly get enhanced insights that feel a bit like "guidance from above" in many cases. Situations where we would have never seen a connection before may suddenly make sense and become totally clear in how they relate to each other. Hence, we can make use of those states of being for our own good. For example, we can connect to the inner self—you may call it intuition—to confirm important decisions in our life. We have the chance to find the missing link to the formula we have been thinking about for so long. We can understand why we acted in a certain way in a specific scenario in the past. We are finally able to feel and understand ourselves and, most importantly, to shape our own future.

My next stop was in Engelberg, a small town farther south. I enjoyed the quiet, the landscape, and especially the view from the Titlis mountain. It was the perfect place to enjoy both the green (in the valley) and the snow (on the mountain). A winter wonderland in spring—absolutely fantastic! During those days, I also participated in a live remote group meditation for the first time. It was a group of people simultaneously participating online in the same guided meditation. The reason behind it is that the intentions and energies of all participants are shared and merged into one big field. While I cannot draw any conclusions about how exactly it impacted my further journey, it certainly was another puzzle piece to what would happen a few weeks later.

I went to Interlaken next, as usual, by train. The Swiss railways offer one of the most scenic train networks I have seen around the world. It takes you around the mountains, through the mountains via tunnels, and alongside the azure-shimmering lakes of the country. Overall, an unforgettable experience with breathtaking panoramas; all you have to do is sit and look out of the window. It surely does captivate everyone's heart. Most definitely mine! I didn't read much during my few days there but rather enjoyed the environment itself. One thing that had been on my to-do list for a long time was buying a new rucksack. Over the last two years, I had been using the old one that I had bought more than ten years previously while studying abroad. It was perfect for my purposes until this point but had started to slowly fall apart. I knew that when the point came when I finally bought a new one, it would also mark the end of my travel adventures. It was symbolic of my readiness to reintegrate. While I was strolling through the streets of the city, I noticed a small shop selling all sorts of things, among them a variety of bags. I went closer and immediately saw "the one" standing right in front of me, a dark gray rucksack, perfectly sized and shaped. I picked it up, checked all available pockets, and bought it without a doubt. While this event may sound somewhat trivial, for me, it was one of many signs that I was ready to take the next step, away from traveling to something new, yet to be determined. I had kept this rucksack task until the end, for when I would find the perfect match without actively looking for it, and it had finally found me. It was a comforting feeling; I could trust that I was on the right path.

A few days later I moved on to Bern, a comparably bigger city dotted with historic buildings. After an initial day of exploration, the weather turned quite rainy—the perfect time for me to continue my reading work. First, I went to the university library to progress with my own materials for a bit. Later, I went to the bookstores, where I again found a few great books on exactly my target topics. I picked three, sat down in the chair at the window, and started to read. It was a different way of reading that I had found worked best for me: I skimmed over certain pages by swiftly scanning a few keywords to make sure it was indeed content that I already knew. Then, once I reached the core chapters that interested me, I read word for word, line by line, if needed, multiple times. For me, it was the perfect way to read for hours at a time and to finish a book quickly. On that day, for example, I read a complete medium-length book in around four hours. I felt that my brain was working intensely, that tingling sensation that made its way around my head. After I digested the contents and took a break outside, I continued with the rest. It was pretty intense, to be honest.

I repeated the same procedure for the next two days. The act of reading was not forceful in the sense of me having to work hard or stay motivated to read. No, it was the exact opposite: I practically soaked in the contents with so much energy, attention, and awareness that while reading, I immediately consolidated my existing knowledge and new understanding of those aspects. I didn't even need a lot of repetition, like we sometimes do when bluntly memorizing data or facts for university exams, for instance. It simply clicked and stuck with me on the first attempt. This is what we would typically describe as a flow state; while I regularly had experiences like these before, to a certain degree, this intensity and duration was something singular and also new to me. It was a feeling of limitlessness, that everything was possible. As if I had tapped into a bigger field of energy that I could feed off. It was easy to comprehend and connect the new and old information. It simply made sense. Nobody had to explain anything to me. I got it myself. Here I was, gaining insights from my heightened state of consciousness, practically applying the use that I had wondered about only a few days before. It was powerful.

The days in Bern had passed in no time, and now I was on my way to the next destination, Zurich. While I didn't particularly like the overall atmosphere and looks of Bern, I really loved Zurich. Everything seemed so positive here, each person so friendly, from taxi drivers to kiosk owners and random people on the streets. Most likely, this impression was partially attributable to my general mood of bliss, but the city itself definitely had a really good character to it. I stayed for three days and continued with the same routine: Going to libraries and bookstores to read. For those interested, I was inter alia reading books by well-known authors such as Joe Dispenza, Bruce Lipton, Deepak Chopra, and Gregg Braden—all around the topics of "the power within ourselves", coupling spirituality with science. Of course, I also read many other books and papers covering more specific and technical niches (e.g., physics and biology), but the above names should give an indication of what it was mainly about.

One evening, I was sitting in the common room of my hotel, right at the lake in the historic district of the city. I had a fruitful day of studying behind me and simply sat at the window, watching the people pass by, enjoying my time. I was really grateful for these wonderful weeks in Switzerland. Not only did I enjoy the small villages in and around the mountains a lot, but also my time in the bigger cities, thanks to the available reading material in the libraries and bookstores. The situation was comparable to Austria, where I also found exactly the right material I needed to read on my way, at each stop an additional piece. I sat in the exact same place for around two hours, doing nothing but looking out the window, being totally at peace. The receptionist lady came by to water the plants around me, people came in and out, and someone was playing music in the background—nothing bothered me at all. I was simply in the moment, and nothing could get me out of it. There was nothing around me I was interested in; nothing was of importance. Nothing was more beautiful than this precise position I was in, this perfect meditative state with open eyes.

After a while, a young woman in her early thirties entered the room to eat dinner and drink a glass of wine. First, I didn't pay much attention and continued with my nothingness. Then she got a phone call, and it sounded like it was work-related. While initially I wasn't keen to give up my wholesome moment, I decided to talk to her for a bit; we were sitting in the same room and might as well enjoy each other's company. "Working on a Sunday, huh?" I said with a smile and added, "I know that feeling!"

She laughed and responded, "Yep, unfortunately, that is how it is as a self-employed person." From there on, we continued the typical intro conversation of where we are from and what brought us here. She was from the US, taking a bit of time to explore some new areas of the world, including Switzerland. After a bit of initial chitchat, another guy entered the room. He was in his late twenties, from Croatia, and visiting Zurich with his PhD study group. At first, we were each sitting at our own table in the common room, talking left to right. Then, we all gathered at the middle table. He was drinking a beer, she was drinking her wine, and I was sipping on my water. As it usually was during those spontaneous gatherings, both of them had many questions regarding my travel experiences over the last years. I didn't particularly like to talk about myself that much, but rather to ask more questions about the stories of others, but it was somewhat natural that they were more interested in an "exotic" story such as mine.

I told them about my life while I was working, what made me quit, how I developed and adapted my way of travel over time, and what brought me to Switzerland as a last stop. When I mentioned the death of my dad, both of them also started to openly share their experiences. All three of our fathers had cancer; one of them had healed by now, one of them was in the final stages, and one of them dead. It built the initial bond between us. Step by step, each one of us would share something additional about him- or herself, ranging from past relationships to shortcomings and general views on the world. The energy in the room started to elevate; we got closer with each story we shared. I could clearly feel the wiring of our invisible, non-physical parts above and around us. It was a beautiful moment to share and experience with both of them. Our conversation helped him to get a different perspective on his past relationship that he still wasn't fully over yet, helped her to trust that she would find the right partner to have a family with at the right time and when she was ready, and helped me to understand that I was extremely lucky with S but that I had been very much tilted toward the right-brain side over the last months—in the long run, I would need to also include my left-brain side into the overall equation. We thanked each other for this wonderful get-together and left for our respective rooms.

That night was very helpful for me, as it confirmed that I had indeed properly digested all the new contents that I had either practically experienced or theoretically learned over the last months and years. In my opinion, this is generally one of the best indicators to confirm if one has really understood what they have attempted to comprehend: To replicate and explain the content in simple terms to others. In addition, I realized once more how good it felt to help other people with such simple things as offering a new perspective on a specific situation or life in general. Sometimes that is all we need, a different perspective, to overcome our old and narrow thinking patterns with their attached negative emotions. The next morning, I woke up highly energized and went down to the common room to get a coffee, where I met the young woman from the night before. She was busy on her laptop, but I came by to say hi, nevertheless. We both felt that the strong bond from the previous night was gone—while last night we had felt like old friends that shared their deepest secrets with each other, today we were merely acquaintances that had a little small talk. But you know what? That was perfectly fine. Our purpose that night was to find and bond with each other so that each one of us could take away important lessons for their future. What was today didn't matter—last night was what would shape our respective paths! Interestingly, it was almost comparable to one of those nights at a bar or club where we make many new "best friends" but forget them all by the next morning. Maybe those two scenarios are not so different after all; both have a certain therapeutic effect.

The next morning, I walked around Zurich one last time, still feeling the bliss and beauty of last night. Over the previous months, I had developed an occasional habit of looking people (who are passing me) directly in the eyes while being in those higher states of consciousness. It was always fascinating to see that a few of them, most likely having had some form of enlightenment themselves, were immediately able to recognize that something was going on. They would look me deeply in the eyes, for much longer than usual when passing a stranger, and couldn't let off until the last second. They knew there was something, but they couldn't figure out what it was. Somehow, they must have sensed my elevated energy level, maybe even subconsciously, but they definitely did. For me, it was a confirmation that what I had learned and practiced seemed to indeed work, that I wasn't going crazy. It was comparable to the following scenario, which I am sure most of us have already experienced in one form or another: You are sitting in a room with other people, waiting for the group to gather and complete. Then, one person walks into the room, and everybody looks up at them. There is something about that person that makes you look up, but you cannot quite figure out what it is. Yes, that is exactly the same thing happening at that moment. You notice their energy, their frequency, their aura—whatever you may call it. You can definitely feel that there is something different about that person that made you look at them while barely noticing all the others who entered the room.

After Zurich, I went to Stein am Rhein, a charming little town surrounded by nature. In the mornings, I took the train to the next city, where I found my favorite reading spot on the first floor of the public library. Luckily, it also had quite a good variety of books fitting my topic. I carefully selected a handful of them and began to read. The first few days, I skimmed through most of them and could gather some selective additional knowledge. After I returned home, I would listen to some more audiobooks and podcasts concerning my topics. I felt that I came closer to understanding how everything was related. Piece by piece, I put together the individual bits of knowledge to form a plausible new paradigm that I was willing to accept. I gradually digested the new information: How everything is energy at its core, how we are all connected via cosmic consciousness, how everyone and everything (humans, animals, plants, objects) constantly vibrates at their or its own frequency, how time is an illusion with past, present, and future all simultaneously existing in wave-form, how each possible scenario of everything that has ever happened and will ever happen already exists and is just a matter of probability, and that we are eventually the creators of our own reality.

Those topics are, at first, a hard pill to swallow. Let us be honest, unless you are a sophisticated philosopher or gifted quantum physicist, the chances of us encountering those topics during our daily life are basically zero. While we can observe an increasing trend of people moving away from traditional religion and looking for liberation elsewhere, there is no proper school-like setup yet where we would be taught such things. To date, each one of us has to take the initiative to gather the required material that will bring us to the decisive, profound aha moment. Sources of information can be books, papers, digital recordings, conversations, or live seminars. All of those are available to anyone who is able and willing to bring the required time and money to the table. Not always an easy task, especially in a world where most of our family, friends, and colleagues will have likely never heard of these topics. Nonetheless, I was lucky enough to find the right material at the right time, which brought me to my second enlightenment.

It was the last day of the month, April 30, 2023, and I was on my way to the library to read. I had put three books onto the shelves that I wanted to tackle that day. When I arrived and was about to grab the books, I noticed another one standing next to them. I had not seen it before, but for some reason (that should not come as a surprise by now), I grabbed the book to see what it was. It had a somewhat confusing title in this translated German version, but I was curious, nevertheless. I took all of them and sat down at the table, put the other three books to the side, and started with the mystic exemplar. The book seemed to perfectly summarize all the content I had gathered from various sources over the last weeks in a crisp and concise manner. I read the book from the beginning to the end with full focus. Again, I felt my brain working extremely hard on both sides, left and right. From my perspective, that is what happens when we actually fire and wire, link and sync new information into our belief systems. It is a process of repetition that can take days or weeks, starting mostly on the right-brain side that allows us to openly approach those topics without pre-judging them with logic and analysis, and later moving on to the left-brain side where we accept the new paradigm as a fact. It is a complete reprogramming of the mind.

The brain is working at its maximum capacity during these moments, needing a substantial amount of energy. However, while being highly conscious, we are able to tap into the cosmic energy field that provides us with the required resources to properly digest the new information, to make the required neuronal connections in the brain, and to anchor the new belief system in our minds. Imagine you need to overwrite years or decades of old beliefs within a few weeks—of course you will need some form of additional resources that help you with the execution and integration. That is exactly what happened to me while I was reading the book. Suddenly, everything became totally clear. I could accurately connect all those different bits and pieces that I had previously gathered, and finally, I had this one source showing me that I was right. Each line was so precise that it almost exactly described how I had felt and acted over the last week. Each explanation matched precisely what I had concluded before without having a definitive confirmation. The big picture became complete; this book was the final missing piece for me to close the loop. I could finally accept the new paradigm as a fact, as it had evolved from an abstract theory to an actual belief of mine.

After I finished reading, I closed my eyes, became still, and simply sat in silence at the library table for the next twenty minutes. It was a relief. I could finally let go. That feeling from the previous weeks that I was close to something was right. I had to have this exact experience at this exact time. Read this exact book at this exact place. Nothing was coincidence. Everything was written. It was perfect. Once again, I saw the magic of the universe unfolding right in front of my eyes. Thank you!

I felt partially euphoric and partially exhausted. I knew from deep inside me that this was it. I didn't need to read anything further. I had learned what I had to learn, digested what I had

Two Years

to digest, overwritten what I had to overwrite. I closed the book, took a picture of the cover as a reminder, and put all four of them back onto the shelves. I was loaded with energy and had to go outside for a few minutes to catch my breath. A few deep, relaxing breaths. My brain was still on fire, tingling sensations all around, but I could slowly calm down and release some of the ample body load. Afterward, I packed my things and took the train home. I needed to lie down and rest. I could feel that a rather strong headache was on its way. What a day! And did you notice something? I had my first enlightenment in Austria and my second one in Switzerland—both neighboring countries to Germany. Austria was on March 31, 2022, while Switzerland was on April 30, 2023—exactly thirteen months apart, each on the last day of the month. In that moment, I didn't know what those similarities could have meant, but I was certain that I would find out when the right time came.

So, that was it. My second enlightenment process had just happened; the next profound aha moment that made me see the world from a completely new and different angle. While my first enlightenment helped me to rediscover my true essence, the everlasting consciousness or the soul, this second enlightenment helped me to understand that at the elementary core, we are all made of the same tiny particles constituting a vortex of energy. Hence, at the subatomic level, we are all energy. Energy that can neither be created nor destroyed but only transformed—everything already exists in the form of energy. Energy that transmits information. We are constantly radiating electrical charges from our thoughts and magnetic charges from our emotions, thereby creating an electromagnetic field around us, ideally in brain and heart coherence. We are never not communicating on the quantum level. It happens all the time, perpetually, twenty-four-seven—we are just not able to perceive it with our typical five senses. Hence, depending on our own thoughts and emotions, the frequencies we are emitting may be higher or lower and will only match with the most probable equivalent in the field. Assuming that each possible scenario already exists in waveform, infinite in combinations, we can go beyond space and time to shape our future.

That means if our thoughts and feelings are mostly negative, we are more likely to go into resonance with likewise negative people, experiences, and circumstances in life. If our thoughts and emotions are positive, on the other hand, we are consequently more likely to encounter such scenarios in our life. To repeat, everyone and everything constantly vibrates at their or its unique frequency. Frequency is the rate at which energy vibrates in the form of waves. Or, to put it differently, waves are vibrations that carry energy, and frequency is a property of those waves: The higher the frequency, the higher the carried energy. Frequency is the language of energy in a certain sense. Therefore, we are more likely to attract what we want in life by sending out a similar frequency. Not only while being in meditation but also during the regular day, while at work, or when out with friends. It is important to remain in brain and heart coherence throughout the day in order to increase the probability of matching the desired outcome. We have to think and feel with conviction, as if we have already achieved what we are aiming for, leaving no room for doubt. What we want, we must become—in the form of frequency. This whole exercise will require a bit of initial work; for some, it may be easier, and for some, harder, but each one has to put in the required effort individually.

With this in mind, I would like to also offer a different perspective on relationships. Do you recall the example I used earlier in the book when I met S from Colombia? It felt like we matched in over 90 percent of all aspects that one would typically regard as important (e.g., sexual attraction, character, patterns and habits, and worldview), while more likely, on average, we would typically categorize our relationships somewhere between 70 and 80 percent, to pick a number. So, what exactly was it that made us feel that strong connection to each other, that she and I had never felt before? It wasn't like we sat together and made a list of similarities and differences; we just felt and knew it. Let us try to approach it in a similar manner as we did in the previous paragraph. Given we are constantly radiating our own thoughts and emotions out in electromagnetic charges, we are more likely to resonate with a partner of similar, or ideally, the same frequency. We have our respective ideals, characteristics, and beliefs that will match with those of our prospective partner to a certain degree. If the overlap is big enough, we will go into resonance with their frequency. It proverbially feels as if we are on the same wavelength—which we in fact are, on the quantum level. It feels as if we are working seamlessly together, and everything flows naturally. We don't need to force anything.

However, now let us assume the plans, desires, or beliefs of one of the partners changes. If the other partner does not transform with them, then the formerly resonating frequencies no longer match. While we were previously on the same wavelength and everything seemed to work so seamlessly, we now find ourselves in increased conflicts, meaningless fights, and diverging interests in life. We then accuse each other of things like "You have changed since I met you," "You are no longer the person I fell in love with," or "I don't recognize you any longer," not realizing what is actually happening at the fundamental, invisible level. Our frequencies have simply changed; our electromagnetic fields are no longer in resonance with each other. While previously it was a wonderful, harmonic interplay of the two, now they are no longer coherent. Likewise, if one partner changes and the other transforms with him, the two fields will stay in resonance. Both partners and, therefore, both sides' thoughts and emotions have transformed together. Despite the changes in patterns and beliefs taking place, we still feel unity. We are still on the same wavelength. In this case, we would say things like "I am so happy that we can always grow together," or "It feels great to define ourselves anew," and will hopefully continue the relationship for many years to come. What we look for in our partner, we must become ourselves as well.

While I don't want to generalize or over-simplify the complex act of love and relationships, let us consider one more example that we can probably all relate to. A couple meets, everything is great in the beginning, they stay together for a few years, and eventually marry. After a while, the two notice that not everything does always work perfectly well, but they know that this is how relationships are. Then, a few years later, they

Two Years

have one or two kids. Their frequencies are highly coherent during that time—both want to be the best parents possible for their kids. It is their common goal to raise them well. The kids grow older, move up the school ranks, and ultimately leave the house to work or study. The kids (young adults) have become mostly independent by now. Next, the couple notices their issues and conflicts with each other becoming more frequent. No longer are they willing to tolerate the shortcomings of the other; while they didn't overemphasize these negative aspects before, they now cannot help but feel they are confronted with them constantly. The few differences didn't play a key role initially, as the couple stayed in resonance thanks to their main purpose of raising the kids. Now that the kids are out of the house, their electromagnetic fields no longer resonate sufficiently—unless both have other shared interests or goals, for example. If the couple cannot transform together from here, a breakup becomes more likely. Their individual frequencies have changed.

Even though we are just beginning to understand what is possible and happening on the quantum level, there is a lot of existing literature on these topics out there. I have named a few well-known authors earlier in the chapter, but you may also find the more niche or technical material on quantum physics insightful, depending on preference. Undoubtedly, we live in an exciting era of transformation, to say the least. Each one of us who has had one or more profound experiences, that proved whatever is happening in the "background" (i.e., on the subatomic scale) actually works, cannot simply go back to the old way of life. One gets hooked. One wants to know more.

One wants to find out what else is possible. One wants to become the creator of their own future, not limited by space and time.

The next day I woke up a bit groggy. The sheer amount of new information taken in clearly had an impact. It was the first of May, and the library was closed anyway, so I could spend the day at home and relax. I went for a long walk alongside the river and reflected on the last day, which, quite honestly, had also scared me a bit. I would now see the world from a completely new perspective, and that was something pretty significant. However, I felt safe and connected and knew that I could trust my path—things had always turned out exactly right for me, and I had no reason to believe it would be different this time. Back at the apartment, I started journaling down a few thoughts for the future. What I had just learned and accepted, I now had to start integrating into my life. It was something material that I would also like to pass on to other people. But how could I do that? I remembered situations like in Zurich (with the young woman and guy in the common room) where I could share selected knowledge in the form of anecdotes. However, it wasn't really a structured approach to reach a broader audience. I also didn't want to become one of the many speakers and seminar leaders that have been flooding the market over the last several years. Then it clicked: The book. Of course, all I had experienced would become a part of my book; it would contain the first enlightenment (rediscovery of the essence) as well as the second one (everything is energy and frequency). With the book, I could reach a broader audience—assuming people would be interested in reading it—and would not have to become a public figure compelled to follow schedules.

I further reflected on the past months of my travels and remembered how good it also felt to help other people in less fortunate financial situations. Not extreme sums of money, but a little support here and there that would help them to buy a meal, new clothes, or school material for their kids. I really enjoyed those moments of sharing, especially in the poorer countries, as they brought them, and in turn also me, so much joy. But how could I combine these two aspects? I wanted to help people around the world on the spiritual level as well as financially. I had taken some sizable financial losses myself just a year ago and certainly didn't have enough resources to support any bigger projects. Then it came to me: How about I donate a portion of the income from the book? And how about I let the readers vote on which projects to support? Yes, this was it! A unique level of reader involvement. Why should I decide which country or project to donate the money to? Why shouldn't the readers decide it? They would know that with each book they buy, they will contribute to a good cause. In addition, each one of them would be involved in the decision process. A new form of print utility and governance. Each book representing one vote.

I was fascinated by the idea and had never seen anything like it before. It was such a beautiful construct with a flywheel effect. The more books would sell, the more people would find spiritual support, and furthermore, the more money would be available for financial support. Was it even possible? Were there any legal concerns? That didn't matter for now—what mattered was that I had finally found something that I was excited to work toward that would align with my new values and goals. I had found my new guiding principle, my North Star in life:

I am supporting people in need around the world, spiritually as well as financially.

Totally euphoric, I journaled the new plans and took the rest of the day off. It was time to rest. I called S to tell her about my insights and plans, and she was genuinely happy for me. We had been in daily contact throughout the whole time. Like before, I kept her updated on where I was and what I did, what I read, what I ate, and what I thought—and she did the same. She was still with me; despite the geographical distance and no concrete plan for a potential future, we were closer than ever before.

As indicated earlier, she had her own experiences with these topics and therefore could not only comprehend but also share my views. It was perfect. We were exactly on the same level. We both knew the same and could openly talk about it. No shame or fear, just pure honesty. For example, that night, she told me for the first time that before we matched on the app in Colombia, she noted down on a piece of paper what she was looking for in a man. She wrote down her intentions and related emotions, visualized and felt it happening, and thereby matched with my frequency. She did it around the same time when I had my key night in Guatemala (the last night before flying to Costa Rica), where I manifested to meet my soulmate. It was beautiful; we both understood what had happened and that we didn't meet by accident. It was all driven by our own influence. Without cause, no effect. This realization was another confirmation for me that what I had just comprehended was real—it was not just some spooky witchcraft. Even though science cannot exactly pin down yet how the individual processes happen on the (invisible) quantum level, many of us know from experience that it somehow works. It just doesn't work in the traditional scientific sense of "each try yielding the same results". It's highly individualistic and subjective instead. Therefore, many scientists, while acknowledging there is something deeper going on, still oppose recategorizing it from spirituality to science. However, the views are at least slowly starting to change. After our discussion, I went to sleep in peace, as I would be making my way back to Zurich the next day.

Here I would also like to anecdotally mention the ravens that I saw everywhere I went in Switzerland, similar to how I had seen them in Austria the year before. Without me actively looking for them, they just appeared in almost every location I stopped at. Over me, next to me, in front of me. It didn't matter if I was on a walk in the mountains or likewise in a valley. They were there. Or if I was standing on a tower overlooking the beautiful landscape. They were sitting in the treetops around me. Once more, it was a beautiful thing to witness, a sign of comfort and guidance on my path.

Back in Zurich, I definitely felt exhaustion setting in. I was still motivated to read more but didn't have the necessary capacity any longer. I felt that I needed a break. I could have pushed and forced myself to continue, but that would have definitely been counterproductive. I took my foot off the gas and enjoyed my free time instead. I walked around the city a lot to determine whether I could imagine living in Zurich long term; after all, I had just had pretty significant experiences there. But I wasn't sure, to be honest. I still didn't know what I wanted to do, work wise, in the future. I hadn't spent any time thinking about it yet. I had been busy with reading, digesting, and implementing. Then it kicked me off my feet with a big burst: What shall I do now in life? Where do I live? What profession? What will happen between S and me? All of a sudden, all the unpleasant questions and thoughts that I hadn't had any time to work on previously were coming over me at once. I felt overwhelmed, and a sense of panic set in. I spent the next few days with mixed emotions. Naturally, my ego-mind, which partially took control again, made me think about potential jobs that I needed to apply to as soon as possible. I tried to think about what I would like to do going forward but could not grasp a clear thought. It was pure chaos in my head. After the past weeks of highly conscious states full of trust, intuition, and love, I suddenly was confronted with the ego-dominant characteristics of control, overthinking, and fear. After I had just so conclusively developed my future book concept, it suddenly seemed a rather naïve idea.

I also started doubting my relationship with S: Would it ever work anyway? What if I have a fixed office job again? Will we even see each other regularly? Do I really love her? Am I just attached to a romantic dream instead of reality? My previous clarity was gone, and I was completely confused. I couldn't make up my mind in that short amount of time. I called S to talk with her about it and obviously also infected her with my doubts. We both felt the pain. We didn't know what to do. After a day of silence, we talked again and confirmed that we indeed wanted to be with each other, despite not knowing the practical details of what this relationship could look like in the long run. We remembered that what had always worked best for us in the past was just following the natural flow, not forcing anything, and not planning long-term (yet). At that point in time we couldn't make any fixed plans and most certainly could not control the outcome of this situation. I wasn't used to such an overflow of (old) thinking patterns anymore, and hence it took me a while to take my ego off the driver's seat. I decided that I needed to see her in order to make a proper decision. If I didn't go see her now, I would most definitely go my own way and likely never see her again. If I went to see her now, I could at least confirm what was between us was real and then take it from there. I booked a flight to Bogotá for the next day.

On my flight, I sat next to a young woman from Colombia. We started talking, and it turned out she had just come from Germany, where she lived with her German husband. The two had met around ten years ago in Colombia and started a somewhat loose long-distance relationship for around two years. She sometimes visited him; he sometimes visited her. Until one day, he asked her to marry him—then she moved to Germany. It wasn't easy for her in the beginning. She had to learn the language (she was pretty fluent by now), had to find work, and had to find her own circle of friends. However, she managed to do all that, and a few years later, the two of them also built a house together. Nevertheless, it was now their seventh year of relationship, and they were in a crisis period. He seemed to be distancing himself from her; she wanted him to include her more in his life. The typical death spiral of push and pull in many relationships. She was on her way to meet her parents to get a few weeks of time for herself. Both of them wanted to think about the relationship and whether they could see a way forward. I listened to her story and then told her mine, that S and I were practically the "earlier version" of them—pretty much in the beginning phase.

Do you remember when I said earlier that everything had been working in our favor when we initially met? For example, she had the exact matching days off from the hospital or just had finished her exams, always when I came to see her. The above encounter with the other Colombian woman was another of the many synchronicities that we had faced on our way, and there were quite a few. All those little signs and situations popping out of nowhere, all these seemingly coincidental circumstances that helped us on the way to what was likely meant to happen. The young woman's story was a good reminder that everything was possible but that the way was not always easy. The two had bridged several years over long distance before actually marrying and moving in together. Then, both were naturally faced with the usual issues any other couple would face over time. Was it worth all the trouble in the end? Can one even assign a value to relationships and love? S and I would have to find out.

Once I landed, S and I were naturally happy to see each other. It felt good to be with her again. We really did miss each other.

Two Years

This strong bond that had been forming between us made it hard to forget the other person and to simply let the rational self continue with daily life in our respective home countries. While S was at work, I continued collecting my thoughts for the future. I also thought about my book—while I had been so convinced about the idea during my highly conscious states, I had begun to doubt and scrutinize the plans over the past few days. Was this book really something worth writing? What was so special about my story anyway? What if I just wasted my time with it? However, a while later, I relistened to an old recording that I had saved on my phone, which had always helped me when I was in phases of doubt and despair. And it didn't let me down this time either! While listening to it, I regained the required confidence, got up immediately, and wrote down all the features that, from my perspective, would make this a great book. I was convinced again that it should work. The reader involvement or "print utility and governance" part was what I was especially excited about. If I were a reader, I would love to be involved and feel like a part of the overall story. And with my book, each reader indeed had the chance to become a part of something unique.

I sat down, opened my laptop, and started detailing the initial rough outline that I had written a few weeks earlier in the taxi to Antigua. I wanted to progress; I had the required motivation and conviction. I typed for several hours straight, paused, and felt that I'd gotten it. I was in the right mindset to pin down a proper structure and concept. Now, all I had to do was write—fill the blank pages with content. When I told S about it, she wasn't really sure yet if it was just a random idea of mine or if

I really meant it, but she was happy for me, regardless. The next day we went on a short weekend trip into nature together.

We had booked a room in a family house around two hours outside the city. And here we had another encounter or synchronicity that would point us directly toward the unlimited possibilities. The parents were still living in the house, but the daughter, in her early thirties, had met a German guy a few years back, married him not long ago, and lived with him in Germany now. They told us that we reminded them so much of their own daughter and her husband and handed us homemade bracelets in the colors of the Colombian and German flags as gifts to symbolize that everything was possible. Something out there was clearly telling us to continue our path together. However, I was still caught up in my thoughts about the future —yes, the book idea was great. But at some point, I also had to work "properly" again, I thought. I really did not see myself as a professional author. After all, I had never written anything meaningful besides my bachelor's and master's thesis and two papers, and that was a long time ago. On the other hand, whenever I thought about being in a fixed office environment again, I felt constriction and discomfort. It just didn't seem right. I could have literally picked anything and would have done fine with it in the end, but now I had the chance to really find something unique that would fit my new way of seeing and approaching the world. I was completely free to choose anything I wanted. A blessing and a curse at the same time. Given I could not decide what I was actually looking for, I decided to try another way—instead of thinking about concrete jobs as an end result, I decided to start from the traits and characteristics that my future job would ideally have, at least partially.

I practically applied my newly accepted paradigm: Anything can—with a higher probability—be drawn toward ourselves with the right intentions and related emotions. It was a moment of pure clarity. If I couldn't decide what I wanted, why shouldn't I leave the key criteria with "someone" else and let that someone come up with an idea? Someone who had been with me the whole time, who guided me through all those ups and downs, who helped me to keep going when it was rough— the universe. I would give up control and open myself to anything that came. Maybe there were opportunities out there that I would never have thought of by taking the traditional routes. And maybe those opportunities would arise in a completely atypical way. Of course, everything was possible. I had literally nothing to lose. I had to try. I wrote everything down, sat in meditation, and radiated my intentions and emotions into the field. That was it (for now—I repeated the same exercise multiple times over the following weeks). I had to let go of the situation, trust that the right opportunity would show up, and be ready to receive it when the time came. Let go, trust, and receive!

After we returned to the city, S and I talked about our potential future together. We had to face those unpleasant questions at some point. We had become so close by now that it was not just a holiday romance any longer; we had honestly fallen in love with each other. It was hard—she was rather inflexible, location-wise, for the next two years. I wasn't sure where I would be in a few months. Obviously, it wasn't a particularly great conversation. Nevertheless, one of our shared characteristics was that we were totally honest with each other—I really loved that about S. With her, I could always be honest, no matter the point of discussion. We could talk about things in a mature manner. We did that also now. We discussed that maybe our experience was only meant to be for those few months, that we had been fated to meet to help each other grow, that our paths were meant to diverge from here onwards, and that we maybe should try to stay friends. Every time we took a long-term perspective, things seemed rather impossible. There were too many unknowns to make a proper plan. It was a chicken and egg situation. Annoying! We agreed that we should take it a bit slower and remain in contact occasionally, but not as intensively and regularly as before. Thereby, each one of us could focus on our respective to-dos without prejudice. We could see day by day how we felt about the situation and adapt accordingly, if and where needed. That was all we could come up with at that point. We said goodbye with a lot of uncertainty, a situation that hurt both of us.

It was mid-May by now, and I had to fly home to Germany, as my friend's wedding was around the corner. I spent a few days at home progressing with my book, checking if my old suits would still fit me after two years on the road, and preparing my best man speech. The event was great—it was good to see my old friends from my working days, exchange stories with each other, and have a few drinks together. The whole wedding was a success; definitely a day to remember. It was interesting to see how everyone had gone their own way over the last years, how the worldviews differed in terms of narrowness or openness, and how divergent the level of seriousness toward life in general was. I confirmed for myself that life is a series of choices, that there is no right or wrong, and that anything can happen at any time that might completely shake up whatever we believe we are in control of. I was happy, I was comfortable, I was free.

After the wedding, I rented an apartment in a small town in Germany, where I wanted to focus undistractedly on writing the book. Indeed, I wrote for hours each day; it flowed and felt easy. My hands were once again practically typing automatically, as if being guided. All the contents that had been stored in my mind for months finally found their way onto the blank pages. I could write for days without any interruptions and progressed very well. I set myself the goal to finish the book as much as possible by the first week of June, as I still had an old flight to Colombia booked for that time. But S and I hadn't been talking as much over the last two weeks. I wasn't sure if I should still go to see her or try to leave this chapter behind. What should I do? Was I once again limited by my fears? Or did I finally accept that our time together was always meant to be finite? I didn't know yet, but I would have to figure it out soon.

Here I am, at the end of May 2023, writing the last lines of this book. This personal piece of mine that I hope will help and inspire other people on their journey to whatever they may be longing for. Trust in yourselves. Trust that everything will be all right. Trust in the higher power in and around each one of us. Trust in the universe! For me, the unique time of travel and transformation is over for now. A time of becoming free from all conditioning, old patterns, and narrow beliefs. I learned so much about life during that period and am eternally grateful for everything that has happened. I really wish I could tell you how my life continued from here, but for now (!), I have a framework to stick to: Two years.

Closing Remarks

The last two years have been truly transformational for me. It is hard to pin down which event or experience had what specific effect on me and my views on life in general. It is rather the sum of all those things together that make a person grow along the journey. For me, the difference between the "old" me two years ago versus the "new" me today is significant. And that is also the feedback family, friends, and even complete strangers give me. Statements or questions such as, "You seem wise for your age," "How do you know all these things?" "I wish I could do the same," or "If I did not have to do X, I could do Y," are among the most common things I hear when talking to people. It is not like I am forcing my story on them, but I am rather willing to answer any potential questions they might have. Because I was in their shoes just two years ago. I was making the same excuses they are making. I was practically them. Yes, not everybody can simply quit their job and go on a wild run. Though everyone should always be honest with themselves when evaluating what is actually going

Closing Remarks

on: Are you really limited by whatever circumstance you think you are? Or is it rather your fears that hold you back?

We should keep in mind that change is always possible, albeit with certain degrees of variation. If and how we eventually approach it is entirely up to us. There is at least *something* we can do. Sometimes things have to get worse before they get better. Sometimes everything seems to go wrong, only to later turn out to be the most beautiful thing that could have ever happened. It is our own judgments and ego-driven thinking patterns that we need to overcome on our way to liberation. It wasn't an easy path for me either, but I am grateful for everything that has happened, including the seemingly bad things. Those situations can sometimes teach us the most valuable lessons for life, force us out of our comfort zones, and, more importantly, make us feel comfortable in discomfort. Why not let go of the tight plans for a bit? Why not be open to seeing if there is more out there? Why not face our fears and shadows? Why not rediscover who or what we truly are? Why not live to our true potential! We have to give up the illusion of control.

Among the most common questions I get is what my key takeaways from those two years of travel are. Below, I have listed a few for the interested reader:

- We can only understand life looking backward.
- Live by intuition, learn to listen to your inner self.
- The (ego)mind should be used as a tool, not the other way around.
- Our existing belief systems are often rather narrow.

Closing Remarks

- We form the majority of our patterns and habits in childhood.
- Love yourself no matter what, then you can also love others.
- We should feel gratitude each day.
- Family is utterly important.
- The only way out of fear is through the fear.
- When we can't find meaning in life, we distract ourselves with pleasure.
- The privilege of our lifetime is to rediscover who or what we truly are.
- Real transformation means the caterpillar becoming a butterfly.
- We are the creators of our own reality.
- Everything happens at the right time.
- Giving time, attention, and money away is very rewarding.
- The more we heal, the more we detach.
- We have to accept what we cannot change.
- Judgment of good or bad is illusory.
- The ego wants to control, the soul simply trusts.
- Each person we meet mirrors our own shortcomings.
- Silence is the best teacher.
- Soulmates do exist.
- Everything is energy and frequency at its core.
- Books are a tool to release our inner wisdom.

In the end, life is a series of choices resulting in a series of events that will lead us to the same result, one way or the other: Death. The question is how we want to live it until then.

Closing Remarks

Each one of us makes our own choices. There is no "one way" to live. However, we undeniably live in changing times. People around the world are waking up, deeply feeling that there must be something else beyond our life from the ego-perspective. Something that unites us all. Something that we cannot measure, control, or replicate yet. Something that constitutes our true essence. Our life force.

I sincerely hope this book will help or inspire those seeking answers on their journey through life. For me, it has become elementary to support other people wherever possible—no matter their gender, their age, or their ethnicity. The reward from giving is so much more profound than from taking; the shared emotions of joy, satisfaction, and love are among the key "profits" one can make this way, and in my opinion, are much more valuable than anything material could ever offer. Without love, we are practically just an empty shell. Love is crucial for all of us. Love is the universal language of the world. Loving ourselves and loving others are equally important. Of course, it is not always easy to like everyone and multiples harder to feel love for them. But it is not impossible. We just have to relearn, one by one, that we are essentially all the same. We are all connected on a deeper, invisible level beyond our physical bodies. There is no you versus me; there is only us. There is only oneness.

Can we really stop wars with more education? Or rather, more love? Can we really stop racism with more rationality? Or rather, more love? Can we really stop child labor and other unethical behaviors with facts and figures? Or rather, more love? I thought about all these questions for a long time, and for me, the conclusion is clear: The way to make this world a more peaceful place is not via education, rationality, or logic. It has to come from love! Each individual has to learn to love again—themselves and others. We have to stop feeding the ego-self and start reconnecting to our source instead. My proposal forward is as follows:

- Rediscover individually who or what we truly are,
- Realign our values and beliefs as a divine collective, and
- Rebuild society based on these new paradigms.

There is a way out!

Closing Remarks

The book contains a QR code and passcode with which you will have access to vote on the website: www.two-years.com. Let us jointly support the people in need around the world. Every vote counts!

Welcome to a new era of print utility and governance.

Scan QR code to open the voting site

Enter passcode to access the site
Mt34cR21Si69

References

1. Lembke A., 2021, *Dopamine Nation: Finding Balance in the Age of Indulgence.*
2. Levine P. A. and Frederick A., 1997, *Waking the Tiger: Healing Trauma.*
3. Levine P. A., 2005, *Healing Trauma: A Pioneering Program for Restoring the Wisdom of Your Body.*
4. Jung C. G., 1996, *The Psychology of Kundalini Yoga: Notes of Seminar Given in 1932 by C.G. Jung.*
5. Krishna G., 1997, *Kundalini: The Evolutionary Energy in Man.*
6. Jirakittayakorn N. and Wongsawat Y., 2017, *Brain responses to 40-Hz binaural beat and effects on emotion and memory*, International Journal of Psychophysiology.
7. Sharpe R. L. S., Mahmud M., Kaiser M. S., Chen J., 2020, *Gamma entrainment frequency affects mood, memory and cognition: an exploratory pilot study*, Brain Informatics.
8. Clements-Cortes A. and Bartel L., 2022, *Long-Term Multi-Sensory Gamma Stimulation of Dementia Patients: A Case Series Report*, International Journal of Environmental Research and Public Health.
9. Wise A., 2002, *Awakening the Mind: A Guide to Harnessing the Power of Your Brainwaves.*
10. Robbins J., 2008, *A Symphony in the Brain: The Evolution of the New Brain Wave Biofeedback.*

Milton Keynes UK
Ingram Content Group UK Ltd.
UKHW010732300424
441987UK00001B/2

9 781961 532656